MW01026317

**The Arnold and Caroline Rose Monograph Series
of the American Sociological Association**

Paradoxical harvest
Energy and explanation in British history, 1870–1914

Other books in the series

J. Milton Yinger, Kiyoshi Ikeda, Frank Laycock, and Stephen J. Cutler: *Middle Start: An Experiment in the Educational Enrichment of Young Adolescents*

James A. Geschwender: *Class, Race, and Worker Insurgency: The League of Revolutionary Black Workers*

Paul Ritterband: *Education, Employment, and Migration: Israel in Comparative Perspective*

John Low-Beer: *Protest and Participation: The New Working Class in Italy*

Orrin E. Klapp: *Opening and Closing: Strategies of Information Adaptation in Society*

Rita James Simon: *Continuity and Change: A Study of Two Ethnic Communities in Israel*

Marshall B. Clinard: *Cities with Little Crime: The Case of Switzerland*

Steven T. Bossert: *Tasks and Social Relationships in Classrooms: A Study of Instructional Organization and Its Consequences*

Richard E. Johnson: *Juvenile Delinquency and Its Origins: An Integrated Theoretical Approach*

David R. Heise: *Understanding Events: Affect and the Construction of Social Action*

Ida Harper Simpson: *From Student to Nurse: A Longitudinal Study of Socialization*

Stephen P. Turner: *Sociological Explanation as Translation*

Janet W. Salaff: *Working Daughters of Hong Kong: Filial Piety or Power in the Family?*

Joseph Chamie: *Religion and Fertility: Arab Christian–Muslim Differentials*

William Friedland, Amy Barton, Robert Thomas: *Manufacturing Green Gold: Capital, Labor, and Technology in the Lettuce Industry*

Paradoxical harvest

Energy and explanation in British history, 1870–1914

Richard N. Adams

Cambridge University Press

Cambridge
London   New York   New Rochelle
Melbourne   Sydney

Published by the Press Syndicate of the University of Cambridge
The Pitt Building, Trumpington Street, Cambridge CB2 1RP
32 East 57th Street, New York, NY 10022, USA
296 Beaconsfield Parade, Middle Park, Melbourne 3206, Australia

First published 1982

Printed in the United States of America

Library of Congress Cataloging in Publication Data

Adams, Richard Newbold, 1924–

Paradoxical harvest.

(The Arnold and Caroline Rose monograph
series of the American Sociological Association)

Bibliography: p.

Includes index.

1. Great Britain – Economic conditions – 19th
century.   2. Great Britain – Economic con-
ditions – 20th century.   3. Energy consumption –
Great Britain – History – 19th century.
4. Energy consumption – Great Britain – History –
20th century.   5. Economic history.   I. Title.
II. Series.
HC255.A57   305'.0941   81–21631
ISBN 0 521 24637 7 hard covers   AACR2
ISBN 0 521 28866 5 paperback

Contents

Figures and tables

Figures

Tables

Preface

The notion that human society can expand and become more complex only in some direct relationship to the amount of energy that it consumes has been long argued and is being accepted by an increasing audience (Cottrell 1955, Sahlins 1960, White 1943). The discussion of the relevance of this proposition to a better understanding of social organization has generally been shunted aside. The present study is the first part of an inquiry into that general subject.

As an outgrowth of a more general inquiry into the relationship between energy and society (Adams 1975), I wanted to explore the history of a complex society to see more precisely in what ways the amount of energy used affected the nature of the social structure. My first examination was the history of Spanish America; I had worked there and had an initial familiarity with the sources. After a year of searching through the materials covering the first two centuries of its history, I regretfully concluded that the primary research had not yet been done in sufficient depth to make it profitable to explore the kinds of problems I had in mind. In many social histories, the authors have created social analyses at the same time that they were patching together the history that was used to sustain their arguments. I preferred not to become involved in primary research but to rely on the work of historians and other analysts. Ideally, the situation would be one on which a great deal of research had been done and which had aroused many controversial interpretations. The virtue of such controversy is that it helps throw light on distinctive aspects of the events.

I decided to focus on British history of the nineteenth century, on the grounds that a great deal of primary research had been done both on national and local topics, and that much of it had been subjected to searching analyses by a wide range of specialists. In the abundance of material I was not disappointed. Hanham's 1976 bibliography cites some 10,000 primary sources for the period 1851–1914, and of course there were additional articles and more recent work. If work on Latin America was scarce, the problem here was the impossibility of reviewing seriously all the relevant material. Consequently, I followed certain leads and by necessity left others unpursued. Before beginning the work, I spent a month consulting with scholars in Great Britain and received a great deal of help from many individuals in Scotland, Wales, and England. In the course of that visit, I encountered the work of Humphrey and Stanislaw (1979) at the Cavendish Laboratories. One of the important features evident in that work was the leveling off of per capita energy consumption in the latter part of the nineteenth century and its fluctuating, quasi–steady-state condition for the first half of the twentieth century (Figure 3.1).

My interest immediately focused on the period 1910–50. There has been much discussion on the possibility of a steady state in the future of humanity, and most of the writing has been either speculative or based on what has been called an economic steady state. The literature has given little attention to the possible consequences of real steady states of an energetic nature. I thought it would be useful to study this period with this question in mind. To do this, however, I realized that it would be critical to first understand why Great Britain had entered such a condition. Presumably, whatever factors had led to that condition would continue to operate for some period thereafter. I had the opportunity to spend a year at the Center for Advanced Studies in the Behavioral Sciences at Stanford, California, and I devoted most of my time there to an exploration of the literature on the period 1870–1914, since that was the era during which the per capita energy consumption leveled off.

Three bodies of material resulted from my work that year. The first was a further theoretical analysis of how to handle energy flows as a part of social phenomena; I have summarized some of that material in Chapter 2 of the present monograph. The second was a series of concepts for dealing with social groups in complex societies that would permit an analysis in terms of energy of the activities of the group and would also relate them dynamically to the process of evolutionary emergence of new societal elements. Portions of this have been presented in Adams (1981). Materials from both these works have been further developed and expanded in a forthcoming theoretical work, *Society as Energy Structure* (Adams in preparation). The final material was an organized body of notes on Victorian Britain aimed at the problem of exploring the so-called decline of Great Britain at the end of the last century. A reworking of this material constitutes the substance of this monograph.

My purpose, then, in this analysis is to suggest a way of looking at the history of Great Britain during the period 1870–1914, from a point of view of energy in society. I have made every effort to keep the material from drowning in a sea of terminology. The ideas that lie behind this analysis, however, are founded on concepts concerning the nature of energy processes, and in order to understand some of the direction the analysis takes, it is probably necessary to have some understanding of these. I have therefore set forth some of these ideas in Chapter 2, illustrating them with British materials. Readers may or may not find that chapter to their interest or liking, but it must be emphasized that it is only there that the use of such terms as "dissipative structure," "flow," and "trigger" are explained.

I have avoided technical terms that I have introduced elsewhere as a means of analyzing the social structure of Great Britain, and I have likewise omitted any consideration of the internal organization of British society. Such an analysis would need to introduce this set of concepts because they contain propositions about the dynamics of society. I would also have to explore aspects of British social history in much greater depth than is appropriate here.

In this monograph I attempt to reevaluate and recast materials already available. Except for material in Chapter 10, no new data will be found here. I depend entirely on primary research already done and on secondary interpretations that I think pertinent. I review events in a context of world energetic and ecological processes. Chapter 2 sets forth some of the assumptions I use; an extended defense of them will appear in Adams (in preparation).

After the manuscript was submitted for publication, various additional works of relevance came to my attention. None affected the argument as it stands, although some throw more light on various historical elements. One, however, by Martin J. Wiener (1981) deals with questions so pertinent to the present work that I rewrote the third section of Chapter 11.

Note on terminology: I have used the term "Great Britain" in preference to "United Kingdom" in several instances where the latter would have been correct. My reason is that there seems to be no adjectival form for the United Kingdom. Wherever one or the other is used with respect to quantitative data, however, the correct term is used.

Initial work on this project was carried out under a fellowship from the Guggenheim Foundation. The major part of the research leading to this monograph was carried out at the Center for Advanced Studies, Stanford, California, while the writer was a Fellow working under grants from the National Endowment for the Humanities (Grant No. FC 26278-76-1030) and the University Research Institute of the University of Texas at Austin. The final manuscript was prepared while I was a Visiting Fellow at the Institute of Advanced Studies, Research School of Social Sciences, Australian National University, Canberra. I owe many thanks to these institutions for the support they provided. I discussed the materials of the present work with a number of individuals. I can identify specific obligations to Dr. Bryan Roberts, Dr. Robert Keohane, Dr. James Rule, Dr. Robert Hauser, and Mr. Anthony King. I am indebted to Mr. Alexander Stewart for creative and

penetrating observations and to Mr. Nicolas Barker, Professor Oliver Mac-
Donagh, and Dr. Henry Selby for very useful commentary on the manuscript. I
owe a special debt to Dr. John Higley for many discussions on these problems
and to his continuing interest over the years. Professor Frank Lancaster Jones
and Ms. Michele Robertson provided much help in preparing the manuscript in
Canberra. Mr. David Knowlton researched British agriculture and his work contributed to Chapter 7. Materials in Chapter 10 were developed at the Australian
National University, and seminars concerning them were given at the ANU, La
Trobe University, the University of New South Wales, the University of Sydney,
the University of Tasmania, and the University of Western Australia. I am grate-
ful to Professor S. B. Saul for permission to use materials in Table 5.1 and to
Professor Mancur Olson for permission to use in Chapter 1 a quotation from his
unpublished manuscript, "The Political Economy of Comparative Growth Rates."
Ms. Beverly Beaty-Benadom and Mrs. Betty Gamble typed earlier and later
drafts of the manuscript; Mrs. V. M. Lyon and Mr. Robert Graham prepared the
figures. I am most indebted to these patient people for their good humor and fine
work. The responsibility for the final form rests with me.

R. N. A.

Austin
December 1981

1. A historical overview, 1870–1914

British population and cultural material expanded at an unprecedented rate in the nineteenth century. Because it was the world's first nation to experience the industrial revolution, Britain, for better and for worse, served as a model for the rest of the world. The British expansion was related to several commonly recognized, important facts. The proximity of iron ore and coal of good quality permitted a conjunction of flow that was not so easily obtained in some other countries. The lack of a land-based peasantry permitted economic pressures to channel labor in ways convenient to those in power. The increase in population kept wages down. Population growth, together with the expanding wealth of the upper and middle classes, amplified demand for home production and imports. This, coupled with an ever increasing need to export manufactures, made Britain highly dependent on the outside world by the end of the century.

Ecology teaches an important general principle about the survival of living systems. Individuals and societies can expect to continue in a viable condition only if their environment remains in a condition that will provide them with the things they need. A society that fails to condition its environment must necessarily eventually come to grips with a decline or disappearance of resources. Societies and environments evolve together, as whole systems (Margalef 1968). As Great Britain industrialized, it could not escape this ecological imperative. It had to have an environment – an international environment – that would be benign to British growth. As the first industrial nation, Britain had either to develop trade, foreign markets, and raw material sources, or it had to cease to expand. In the early nineteenth century the Corn Laws guaranteed that most food would come from domestic agriculture. Recognizing that such restrictive legislation was inhibiting a free trade that was necessary to construct external markets, Britain began in the 1840s to systematically reduce obstructions to exports and

For this survey I relied principally on Aldcroft (1964, 1970, 1968), Ashworth (1960), Beer (1969), Cairncross (1953), Court (1965a), Deane and Cole (1967), Ensor (1936), Habakkuk (1962), Halévy (1951), Hinsley (1962), Hobsbawm (1969), Imlah (1958), Landes (1969), Macdonald (1969), Mitchell and Deane (1962), Saul (1965, 1969), Semmel (1968), Stearns (1969), C. Wilson (1962), and Young (1936), as well as other sources as cited.

imports, and vigorously pushed other nations to emulate its policies. For a few critical decades it was highly successful. Others, wanting Britain's industrial products, fell into line.

By the mid-nineteenth century, laissez-faire and free trade were major planks of British foreign economic policy. Export markets and cheap imports allowed Adam Smith's invisible hand to benefit visibly Her Majesty's kingdom. Free trade was indisputably advantageous to those with capital to exploit pioneer environments by giving an edge over the less well endowed. It worked to British advantage for most of the nineteenth century.

Laissez-faire rationalized other British characteristics of the era. Evangelical fervor polished the British way of doing things with spiritual righteousness. It twisted the principles of evolution into a doctrine that co-opted religion on the side of those who achieved success and conveniently obscured those cruelties that should have embarrassed espousers of the Christian ethic. It was also committed to judging government intervention as an evil, though even classical theorists recognized that if the state were to do nothing in such areas as education and public health, nothing was likely to be done. But for most other areas, the policy was "hands off." This circumspect role of the government rationalized an ability to consider the suffering poor – that other "nation," in Disraeli's terms – to be a necessary, if disagreeable, part of the natural order. The one categorical exception to the policy of government nonintervention concerned the expansion overseas. Outside of Great Britain, it was deemed not only acceptable but at times obligatory for the navy or army to intervene to advance British interests. The foreign environment presented dangers and inhibitions that could not always be expected to yield to the invisible logic of laissez-faire.

Free trade found favor not only with capitalists but with the working class, because the repeal of the Corn Laws brought down the price of food. Indeed, the devotion to free trade was still part of working-class ideology until the depression of the 1930s. But the preference for this policy – which on the surface would seem to benefit only the able and wealthy – went even deeper. Since laissez-faire gave the capitalist and entrepreneur a free hand, one might think that labor would have welcomed measures to promote their interests against the employers and entrepreneurs. This, however, was not the case; government-sponsored welfare measures were often resisted. The reason was simple: The working class had learned through years of experience to be intensely suspicious of efforts by existing institutions to change social policy. Remarkable inventions such as the workhouse were quite enough to show that government intervention was not desirable. This was an era when declining prices meant a steady rise in real wages, and the growth of production benefited the mass market. A wage increase that, in 1870, was enough only to buy some extra beer or gin was, by 1900, buying an increasing array of cheap consumer products.

It seems that British government intervention in the nineteenth century was mainly a mechanism for inhibiting entrepreneurs from destroying each other or for reducing the human, social, and material waste that they were depositing on the national territory. Thus the culture of British government policy was to hinder certain developments, not to promote others. (Contrast this with positive promotions in both Germany and the United States.) This attitude of government was not an invention of government planners but the reflection of an overwhelming British cultural policy. It both reinforced and was reinforced by the wider culture.

With almost total national support, free trade proved to be a capital success until the last quarter of the century. Then the halcyon era felt a shudder. The great export successes were threatened by the accelerating industries of Germany and the United States. A continual fall in prices did not destroy profits, but it obviously cut into them. A series of droughts in the 1870s, accompanied by an avalanche of cheap foreign grains, reduced the British wheat industry by half and led to the conversion of almost a quarter of the arable land into pasture. This in turn contributed to the final economic weakening of much of the aristocracy, and with it came a consistent spread of the franchise. The stern, vocal evangelical morality, that backbone of midcentury Victorian righteousness, was drowned out by other voices. Social studies in London and elsewhere exposed appalling poverty and revealed one-quarter of the population in the very heart of the world's richest and most successful nation to be without sufficient subsistence. Many recruits for the South African War proved to be so undernourished and developmentally malformed that they had to be rejected; poverty that was ignored among the poor now affected the ability of the wealthy to defend themselves. As one historian expressed it, it was an era in which fear took hold: One could not predict when the next crash would be or the next failure; one could not predict whether the government would be able to do anything. Midcentury security faded.

Doubts naturally grew about the benefits of free trade. The free importation of grain was an economic disaster to many farmers – particularly those who were less able. The encroachment of German and U.S. industrial products posed an increasing problem, because those countries did not hesitate to protect their own industries at the same time that they constricted traditional British market areas. Arguments by the emerging protectionist movement were clear: Other European countries were building their own industries, British exports were losing markets, and, above all, foreign imports were contributing to depression in British industry. The wheat industry had all but disappeared, and iron and steel were clearly suffering. "Made in Germany" labels were crowding the retail markets in London and other cities, and the lack of expanding industry was producing unemployment and misery. But for political reasons, no British government dared promote "protection" that would reduce profits for the wealthy and cheap food for the poor.

There was another reason that free trade was not in serious trouble. From the 1820s on, Britain suffered a negative balance of merchandise trade. Yet over the same era the net balance of payments was constantly positive. This positive balance of payments was achieved through "invisibles"; income from British shipping, banking, and insurance services; and, of even greater importance in the latter years, from foreign investment. Many London banking houses had originally been foreign firms with a basic interest in foreign investments, and they never provided fixed capital for domestic investment. The Bank of England's policies were consonant with this orientation. In the 40 years preceding World War I, the foreign component of the total British capital investment increased from 18% to 30%. While domestic investment grew by 80% during this era, foreign investment increased by 250%.

Quite clearly, the development of foreign nations, both through direct investment and through services for the expanding international trade, was a profitable venture for a small sector of British society. This was a very important sector, because its success assured Britain of being able to continue to import more than it exported. The cost, of course, was the real threat to British home enterprises: Those who could not meet the foreign competition, made more vigorous by this foreign investment, suffered. Although British industry was still expanding in some sectors, its relative international position was apparently deteriorating.

Foreign investments also yielded direct benefits by contributing to the foreign railways that helped cheap grain reach Britain and by opening the foreign markets where British textiles were sold. This flow of capital was crucial to foreign development, not only in the colonies but in the United States, South America, China, and Europe. As the first industrial nation, there is little question that Britain had to help build those areas that could demand its exports as well as to help develop the foreign capacity to produce the imports it increasingly needed. Quite naturally, the maturation of foreign markets and producers changed them from dependents to competitors. But Britain's pioneering as an industrial market builder and foreign developer was crucial. If Third World nations today argue that this process was uneven, so indeed it was. While Britain's textiles may have prevented full development of such industries elsewhere, it is hard to imagine that Argentina, India, or Australia would have developed their own railway networks without British capital and technology. As Britain lost its advantages in some foreign markets, it moved elsewhere.

Economic historians have disagreed over whether foreign investment was better for Britain than greater domestic investment would have been. But it seems doubtful that there was a very wide choice. If we consider Britain as a society that was expanding significantly – expanding home production, imports, exports, earnings, credits abroad, and population – we must also bear in mind the outside environment that allowed this. Markets do not just appear when goods arrive; and capital is by definition low in underdeveloped areas. In fact, Britain had to create much of this environment. It had to help a world of future competitors build their own capacities. It is quite interesting and, I would argue, important to contemplate what the outside environment would have been without that British investment and service. But just as we can never know how Britain itself would have fared if the investment had been at home rather than abroad, so we can never know just how the world would have fared. To ask the question suggests that it needs more attention. After all, by 1914, Britain had some £4,000 million invested overseas.

The British laissez-faire phenomenon has been discussed widely as a philosophy; it has also been criticized as not being substantively important, since it was often not observed and became a policy only after it had done its work. Let us look at it in another light.

Laissez-faire was a philosophy, but philosophies can exist only as far as they operate in some sector of society. I cannot here explore why this philosophy flourished. Certainly the role of the monarch was weakened in the seventeenth century, and the British governmental system was not prepared to substitute another center of power, with equally centralized decision making, for the monarch. Of great importance were the final defeat of Napoleon, and therefore the end of an immediate military threat on the Continent, and British dominance at sea. Britain, for the first time in many years, was without the external pressures and threats that usually circumscribe and reinforce the tendency to centralize. (Cf. Adams 1975:208–11, Carneiro, 1970.)

The result was that the level of decision making relaxed to a subgovernmental level, where regional and community decision makers could guide their own efforts. Laissez-faire was no free-floating ideology. It was a policy forbidding both state enterprise and intervention in individual enterprise made uniquely possible by the conditions of the time in Britain. Thus the "capitalism" that Hobsbawm (1969) sees to be typical of the nineteenth century was in some degree particularly appropriate to the British situation in the nineteenth century. This era, in which Britain made the extraordinary surge into full industrialization, was the product of circumstances that were unlikely to occur again (Hinsley 1962).

Matthew Arnold made this analysis in 1869:

As feudalism, which with its ideal and habits of subordination was for many centuries silently behind the British Constitution, dies out, and we are left with nothing but our system of checks and our notion of its being the great right and happiness of an Englishman to do as far as possible what he likes, we are in danger of drifting toward anarchy. We have not the notion, so familiar on the Continent and to antiquity, of *the State,* – the nation in its collective and corporate character, entrusted with stringent powers for the general advantage, and controlling individual wills in the name of an interest wider than that of individuals . . . no aristocracy likes the notion of a State-authority . . . Our middle class . . . dreads a powerful administration which might somehow interfere with it . . . Then our working class . . . sooner than submit to a conscription would flee to the mines. [Arnold 1913:43–4]

Arnold was troubled not because Britain ventured into something new but because of the apparent loss of something old – the exercise of state power. The peaceful nineteenth century allowed Britain to concentrate on trade; it allowed exporters to push for free trade while economists promoted it as a policy of development; and Britain's domination of the oceans made this possible. By the mid-1870s, the illusion was tarnishing and cries for protectionism were increasing. But this nineteenth-century concatenation created a new structure that the New World and continental countries could pursue in their own ways. In Britain it took the form of lowering the level of decision making. Whereas later eras could act more objectively and manipulate existing state controls, industrializing Britain had no previous model. The government could not act before the entrepreneurs invented their future; it could only worry about how to pick up the pieces.

An especially salient factor was that the British Navy both protected against military threats and cared for British shipping. Hobsbawm (1969:135–40) emphasizes how this allowed Britain almost free access to the entire underdeveloped world, both in its formal colonies and elsewhere. It did not face serious circumscription until the latter part of the century. Hobsbawm also argues that the era between the abolition of the Corn Laws in 1846 and the depression of the 1870s was the only ''comparative brief historical period when both developed and underdeveloped sectors of the world had an equal interest in working with and not against the British economy, or when they had no choice in the matter'' (1969:138).

The relaxation that allowed decisions to emerge from lower levels meant that we should expect, saving specific inhibitions to the contrary, that expansion would be attempted at all levels, and this seems to have been the case. Much British commercial and industrial growth began, for example, as expansion of family firms or partnerships. The firm was created to help the family, and family fortunes fluctuated with those of their firms. Many early entrepreneurs were not counted as gentlemen, and the success of the firms helped thrust their owners or their owners' children into that exclusive class.

The fact that the family and domestic unit formed the basis of many firms suggests why certain traits were present: paternalizing, fear of expansion beyond what the owner could handle, reluctance to become involved in alliance, limited capital, and a multiplicity of small firms. History has made it clear however, that the launching of the family firms redefined priorities. The firm was the source of input, so it came first; the domestic unit, and its members, became totally subordinated to the man's decisions about what was advantageous to the firm.

It therefore follows that attitudes and policies were programmed by interests present at the level of the domestic unit, and operational decisions were made less at the level of the nation and more on that of the community or region. The notion of growth and expansion was in some sense perpetuated on a provincial scale. The great firms and industries expanded as something entirely new and had to make their own ideology as they proceeded. Again, we must remember that Britain was the *first* to do these things, and as such had few antecedents on which to model behavior.

Success was followed by competitors both in Britain and elsewhere. Established institutions increasingly had to compete with newer, more innovative ones; the older firms with the younger; the conservative firm with the adventurous. Firms, of course, have technologies, labor forces, and skills, and they can suffer from problems of age and adaptability. Thus, for example, the better-established gas industry inhibited development of electricity; and the well-running textile industry found it impossible to adopt newer machinery (which was instead exported and created devastating competition later).

This is by no means the whole picture, but it is unquestionably a crucial part of it. It also conforms in an interesting way to a larger picture of ecological succession. Not only did the firms become established, and in a sense thereby use increasing portions of the flow for their own maintenance, but the other sodalities and infrastructural elements expanded and occupied new places, and constituted an increasingly large demand on the total input for their maintenance. As the century wore on, therefore, the amount diverted from investment and savings into infrastructural processes substantially increased (Ashworth 1960:43–4). This also led to contention over controls and increasingly clogged the power structure with unsolved confrontations, bankruptcies, and other institutional failures.

Olson argues that the emergence of these groups tends to be inhibiting:

The accumulation of narrowly based common-interest organizations will have substantial adverse affect on the rate of the growth of an economy – mainly because of evolutionary implications for the development of that economy . . . Highly encompassing organizations will prefer policies which were less restrictive of growth than common-interest organizations or collusions that control only a negligible proportion of the resources in a society. [Olson n.d.]

In formulating this argument, Olson considers the British case and argues that it conformed to his expectations. Barnett asserts that "by 1914 the British industrial system had been finely parcelled out like peasant allotments between a myriad vested interests, trade union and capitalist. It presented a positively medieval picture of complicated private and corporate customs and privileges hardened by time into absolute right legalistically defended" (1972:89).

In a rather peculiar way, the last third of the nineteenth century witnessed a kind of "battle of Britain," conducted by the emerging contending interests. It was not simply the Marxist contest between the classes – unless "class" is used in the broadest sense – but a battle between different levels of structure, and between different sectors and interests in various degrees of organization. Although World War I was a world affair, it crystallized a stalemate in this uniquely British battle, and a solution came only with the end of World War II. The terrain was untracked for Britain. As the first industrial power, Britain came first in making the profitable decisions, but it also came first in making mistakes.

Observers of late-nineteenth-century events in Great Britain are not of a single opinion. Among recent historians, Hobsbawm notes, almost with nostalgia, that "earlier in the nineteenth century, Britain had certainly not lacked that acute, even irrational, joy in technical progress as such, which we think of as characteristically American" (1969:186). Young sees the new culture as a failing:

Fundamentally, what failed in the late Victorian age, and its flash Edwardian epilogue, was the Victorian public, once so alert, so masculine and so responsible. Compared with their fathers, the men of that time were ceasing to be a ruling or a reasoning stock; the English mind sank toward that easily excited, easily satisfied state of barbarism and childhood which press and politics for their own ends fostered, and on which in turn they fed. [1936:187]

Halévy emphasizes a different aspect of the new Britain:

Whatever the improvements made in her national institutions, England felt an increasingly powerful conviction that her vitality was less than that of certain other nations, and that if she was progressing, her rate of progress was less rapid than theirs – that is to say, if not absolutely, at least relatively to her rivals, she was declining. It was this loss of confidence which explains the far-reaching change in her foreign policy which took place toward the end of the nineteenth century . . . We also witness the decline, if not of England herself, at least of the ideal which she has pursued for an entire century and which she had come to regard as the secret of her greatness – decline of that individualist form of Christianity in which Protestantism essentially consists – and a revival of Catholicism, or, more generally, of the Catholic forms of Christianity . . . I shall inquire whether it was not accompanied by a phenomenon of far deeper significance, a decline of the Christian faith, and should not be regarded as in certain respects its "euthanasia." [1951:viii–ix]

Barnett (1972) also notes the "moral force" and "righteous indignation" that marked British midcentury behavior in world affairs as well as at home; he differs from Halévy in that he sees in it a reason for Britain's weakness, however, not strength.

The loss of evangelical fervor and of faith in general in part reflected an increase in the level of living of the period. Yeo, in his study of Reading at the turn of the century, reports not only a sharp drop in attendance at church but that participation in many of the voluntary organizations changed in the latter part of the century. "The shifting of the centre of gravity of leisure activity away from the agency of the chapel or church on to a pan-Reading level was also part of the pattern affecting many other organizations" (1976:200).

The drift toward "anarchy" predicted by Arnold in 1869 is described by another recent writer:

The distinction to be drawn between the preceding years and the final three decades of the century is the presence of a deeply disturbing sense of fear. Although the country was not plunged into revolution, nor submerged by financial ruin, nor even overpowered by atheists, socialists or advocates of free-love, the middle-class imagination was . . . persistently haunted by the fear that these catastrophes were about to come to pass. The old mid-Victorian world, its belief in the rectitude of everyone knowing his or her place, and its robust faith and its own progress, all seemed to be crumbling into chaos. [Harrison 1977:64]

These are general appreciations and quite naturally express as much about their authors as they do about the period. Young is nostalgic for the manly, high-minded, visionary quality; Barnett reflects the military historian's disgust in what he perceives as a weakening in coming to grips with a changing reality. Halévy finds the core of the Victorian success to have rested on the Protestant religiosity, something that he and Yeo recognize to have evaporated or have been destroyed. And Arnold, echoed years later by Harrison and Hobsbawm, sees the perspective of the time to have been a trajectory toward uncertainty and anarchy.

The sinking mind that offended Young was surely misread. The mind of the upper and middle class that manifested the virtues he so admired did not sink; rather, the mind of the lower classes became vocal, literate, open to some level of communication beyond that available at the local tavern. These minds that had suffered both biochemical and intellectual malnutrition enjoyed what can only be seen to be an improvement in the last quarter of the century. Yeo argues (perhaps prematurely) that "from the mid-nineteenth century onwards, a mass leisure industry was coming into being in Britain. Its products ultimately included such items as cheap daily newspapers, the cinema, football, broadcasting, and the car. As a way of 'spending' 'unmortgaged time,' shopping should be included in its post 1880s manifestations: indeed the whole leisure industry ultimately connected with the distribution of commodities'' (1976:310). One need not be a temperance fanatic to see some alternatives to the tavern as an improvement.

If views as to the nature of the alleged decline vary among the contemporaries of the era and among the historians who have examined it, opinions as to its causes have yielded an even more confused picture. Cairncross (1953) observes how very difficult it was to get reliable data on much material of historical importance; he points out that we do not really know how to determine how much capital is in circulation today, not to speak of this earlier era. Saul's (1969) analysis is perhaps one of the most useful because it provides a review of the various arguments used until that time. He concludes his analysis of the so-called great depression of the late nineteenth century with: ''It is apparent that there is no single explanation of Britain's relative decline. We can only bring out the main factors and seek to eliminate those based on poor reasoning or inadequate research'' (1969:51). He also adds a word of caution about the inaccuracy of the statistics on which the economic historians have to depend. C. Wilson observes, concerning this period, that ''economic fluctuations were not in themselves new; what was new was their amplitude and pervasiveness. The inquiry into their causes has proved, more than most economic inquiries, a bottomless well'' (1962:70). Landes's analysis of the era and the problem of the ''depression'' leads him to the similar conclusion that not only will people tend differentially to see one aspect of these processes as being preferable to another, but that they will always continue to do so. For him there is no ultimate solution (1969:356–8).

Court, in a review of Kindleberger's *Economic Growth in France and Britain 1851–1950,* argues that historians restricted their frameworks so as to miss

significant details, which would have put us on the track of more relevant and self-consistent explanations. The other reflection it creates is at the opposite pole from this. For this is that perhaps our explanations have not been sufficiently general. Can long-period economic change be explained in economic terms only, when one considers that it is not output alone which is changing but society too, with all its preconceptions about what output is, why it should change, how it changes . . . It is the failure of partial equilibrium analysis so far to explain the obvious which is Professor Kindleberger's theme. The doubt he leaves us with concerns the limitations of all economic models, divorced from the study of social and political structures, as explanations of the course of economic history. [1965b:432–3]

Court's point is central. If we try to talk about something as extraordinary (even if it is mislabeled) as the "decline" of Britain, surely we are speaking of something that is more than just the "economy" or some minor part thereof. We are, in fact, concerned with a problem that is far too complex to be reduced to the factors usually examined within the framework of a single scholarly discipline.

The literature abounds with efforts to pin the cause of Britain's "decline" on one or another of a myriad of economic factors. Conrad and Meyer (1965:183–220) illustrate a particularly contorted effort to blame it on the failure to maintain export acceleration at midcentury levels; McCloskey (1973) dedicates himself to proving that a single factor – the failure of British entrepreneurialism – was *not* the culprit. Among the more catholic approaches, along with those of Saul, C. Wilson, and Landes, is that of Lewis (1978:112–34), who sees a range of economic options to have been blocked by "ideological traps":

All strategies available to her were blocked off in one way or another. She could not lower costs by cutting wages because of the unions, or switch to American-type technology because of the slower pace of British workers. She could not reduce her propensity to import by imposing a tariff or by devaluing her currency, or increase her propensity to export by devaluing or by paying export subsidies. She could not pioneer in developing new commodities because this now required a scientific base which did not accord with her humanistic snobbery. So instead she invested her savings abroad; the economy decelerated, the average level of unemployment increased and her young people emigrated. [1978:113]

Although Lewis does not cope with the "traps" implicit in some of his factors, his approach is certainly a healthy one and consonant in principle with that developed here.

The following chapters explore several of the themes introduced in the preceding pages. The approach taken, however, derives from specific methodological and theoretical perspectives. Unfortunately for the reader merely curious about the story, it is necessary to review the framework that lies behind this effort, as well as certain aspects of the study of social history and the way explanations have been brought to bear on it. Since the line of argument and occasional references require some understanding of these issues, I ask the reader's patience while we shift our focus to them.

2. Concepts and theory

Energetics and the social process

The framework and conception of this monograph rest in a special concern with an area that I have come to think of as *energetics*. The term is probably an unfortunate one, but it has dominated my usage simply because I have found no other that serves as well. Everything that is of any concern to us has as one of its dimensions a quality of energy. That is, under some set of circumstances it may be able to do work. In a stricter sense, there are conditions of *equilibrium:* states where under given *environments* there is no way that the forms present can do work. Energy forms that have no capability of doing work are of no intrinsic interest except insofar as they may act, as a part of the environment, to affect the operation of those that can.

In industrializing England of the nineteenth century, for example, the increasing use of coal brought to the industrial and urban centers clouds of smoke. This smoke was a form of energy that had little intrinsic capability of doing any more work. It was a part of the entropy of the conversion of coal. The useful part, the heat, also dissipated so that it too was unavailable for any more work. The smoke, however, constituted an environmental element that posed increasing problems. The real solution to this was not found until after World War II, when coal was banned for domestic use in London. This did not occur until petroleum products became available and began replacing coal.

To understand the energetics of a society requires an examination of the events that involve the expenditure of energy. This is another way of saying that it requires that we look at the whole. A great deal has been said about holistic treatments of societies, but few such attempts even pretend that their working definitions were designed to allow for all the factors that might be relevant. For my purposes, the defining characteristic of the "whole" is that all component parts have the quality of being able to "do work," that is, that they are energetic. This notion can be readily misunderstood, because the term "energy" is used today almost entirely to refer to specific commercial forms of energy. My usage is much broader and includes all material things that have the capability of doing work in the physical sense, no matter how large or how small. Thus even a piece of paper has this capability: It can be burned and will release heat. Human beings are energy forms, as are all living things and artifacts of all varieties. It must be remembered, however, that the quality of being "energetic" is merely the defining characteristic of what may be included in our consideration. It does not designate or indicate what may be important about the things considered. We include a piece of paper because it can be burned; its importance may lie in the fact that it contains a House of Commons report that sets in motion a series of events.

It should be clear immediately that this framework is not that used in most so-called energy studies today. The difference is important. Contemporary attention focuses on energy as a dependent variable, on such issues as how to better control it, how to get more of it, how to make more of it available and cheaper. Thus the focus is on what human beings should do in order to manipulate energy. The perspective of the present work regards energy as a set of independent variables. Basically, I want to explore the ways in which societies take on different forms and processes because of the kinds and amounts of energy that compose them. Thus I first consider the nature of the energy forms and processes, and then try to see what this may reveal about social forms and processes. In this monograph, I move only a short way in this direction. My concern with internal structure of the society is limited to those forms and processes that are readily identifiable as playing a specific role of an energetic nature (as will be detailed in the following).

Classical physics categorically separates *matter* from *energy*. This is obviously a useful distinction for many purposes, but it unfortunately obscures some important aspects of energy. Most forms of matter are such that, if placed in a critical environment, their forms would *convert* and yield potential *working energy* in the process. Thus the distinction between matter and energy is one that depends on the stability of the particular form in a given environment. We think of gasoline or petrol as a form of energy because it is usually in a delicately unstable form, ready to ignite with the appearance of a spark – and sparks are fairly common in our environments. Many metals that we think of as stable, however, would also burn if the environment were made hot enough. So, for the most part, the distinction between energy and matter rests on the question of the *stability of the particular form in the environment*.

Coal is a good example of this. It is a fairly stable form of carbon in most environments common to the human species. In order to gain useful energy from it, it must be kindled to a certain temperature and subjected to an appropriate technology that permits us to control the heat it yields and put it to work. Whether or not particular mineral forms are of interest to us depends on whether we have developed a technology for harnessing the energy they contain: whether we can vary their environment to release their energy and put it to work.

Because of this intimate relation between forms of energy and matter, I find it convenient to use the term ''energetics'' to refer to the universe of matter and energy or, more specifically, to that portion of the universe of matter and energy that is capable of doing work or contributing to having work done.

An additional concept often discussed in relation to energy is *information*. This originally was incorporated in the area of energy studies because it was determined in the theory of communication (Shannon and Weaver 1949) that in its transmission, information was lost in accord with the same *law of entropy* that described the loss of organization of physical energy in the course of its conversion described by the second law of thermodynamics. The law of entropy, however, is a statistical statement, a formula, about order in a particular system and the rate of deterioration or loss of that order. It applies to both information and energy. Information has generally been treated as theoretically distinct from energy, and some recent very creative work insists that there is absolutely no connection theoretically between the two areas (Bateson 1979:100–2). The issue is by no means closed, however, since it is not uncommon among physicists to assume, or suspect, that information and energy may one day be incorporated into a single theoretical system (cf. Slesser 1978:55), and in a forthcoming work, I propose a way to do this (Adams in preparation).

From the perspective of the present approach, there is an important relation between information and energy. Information can be carried only by energetic forms. That is, whether we deal with radio waves, sound waves, books, or what you will, communication occurs through the media of energetic vehicles and energy expenditure. How much energy messages and communication systems require is a question of considerable theoretical interest. Every differentiated energetic part or aspect offers the possibility of carrying information. As Bateson (1979:100–2) points out, it is the contrast or difference that counts in these questions. Obviously, writing and radio waves carry messages; but we must equally recognize that the ''appearance'' of thunder clouds also is a message, as is the ''decline'' in the stock market, or a red semaphore ''turning'' green, or the ''discovery'' of a new technology. Every such difference potentially carries information; for present purposes, the potential is realized if these differences are endowed with meaning in the larger system.

In human, and indeed all ecological, systems of energy, we are interested not only in the amount of energy harnessed to do work but also in the varieties of energy forms that are available, since distinctive kinds of energy can do different kinds of work. That is, each energy form requires a technology for converting it in such a manner that it can do work or utilize its differences as information. The particular classification of different energy forms that is of use here reflects the fact that all forms have an ability to do work themselves and to carry information that can impact other systems. Even the most simple human social system combines with working energy a series of *triggers* that release further energy, and the released energy itself may act directly or indirectly to trigger yet further releases of energy. The expansion of life depends on triggers releasing other triggers, acting between organisms and their environment and within organisms themselves. In dealing with energy, then, we must be interested in triggers as well as in the substantive work done. Triggers are inherently *inhibiting mechanisms*. They cannot create a flow of energy. They can only release or inhibit an energy flow seeking a new equilibrium. Thus to speak of triggers as "amplifying" flow is incorrect. The size of a flow is determined by the forms of energy that compose it; triggers can only open the gates, so to speak, so that a flow may reach some part or all of its potentiality.

What we are calling "triggers" refers, of course, to the multitude of intellectual and technological capabilities that human beings have to manipulate the elements around them, to harness and use the energetic forms for their own advantage and survival. They are of interest here for two reasons. First, they are the devices by which energy is released. Second, they themselves require the expenditure of energy. It costs energy to release a trigger, even though it may be relatively little. To construct a system in which there are triggers also costs energy. Since a trigger essentially imparts information, the energy cost of production and release may also be said to be the energy cost of the information.

Whether an energetic form is characterized as being a trigger depends on its actual or potential role. Thus in British coal production the coal itself was the product of a process that was set in motion by many triggers, including human labor. That human labor was, in a prior sense, the product of the domestic unit that provided the food for the individual and was triggered by the income received as wages. The coal that leaves the mines goes on to become a trigger to industrial processes that yield yet other products, and so on. Thus the role of trigger is always relative to the locus in the system and to its relations to the boundaries of given dissipative structures.

I argue in later chapters that a major characteristic of Great Britain was that it exported triggers – triggers that could conceivably have also been used at home to further the domestic circulation of energy there. Instead, these triggers released energy flows elsewhere in the world and specifically contributed to the growth of the United States and Germany as competing structures. The distinction is between those goods and activities that were more or less destined primarily for consumption and those that were to act to release further energy flows elsewhere. Thus textiles exported for clothing were consumed directly. Of course, it may be argued that these textiles enabled individuals to go to work and thereby acted as a trigger for that work. This cannot be denied; but individuals usually eat food and wear clothes whether they are producing something else or not. This is not true with coal that is sold to foreign industries or of money that goes into foreign railways. These are destined (or at least intended) to act as triggers in those systems.

In discussing energy forms, we speak of *structures* and *flows*. These are not two different forms of energy (like matter and energy) but rather two different aspects of any energetic form. The conjunction of a set of different but related energy forms at any particular time may be said to constitute a structure to the degree that the whole is set apart from the environment in some temporally consistent manner. The presence of such a set of energy forms, however, either in stable form or in some state of conversion, can also be said to constitute a flow through time. Thus when we speak of a society as a flow of energy, we mean that there is an assemblage of energy forms that act in ways appropriate to themselves; some are stable, others convert to new forms. But since there can be no creation or destruction of energy (in accordance with the first law of thermodynamics), we can say that these changes constitute a flow of energy, the structure of which has changed in certain ways. One inevitable component is the loss of energy in the structure to entropy.

It is in observing social organizations that this issue of flow and structure becomes interesting. The British government in the early nineteenth century was composed primarily of Parliament, the government, and the monarch. As the century wore on, the government and Parliament found that an increasing number of demands were being made on them. This led to the gradual expansion of activities, which in turn required an introduction of new roles and the individuals to fill them. If a *regulatory* operation of the state consisted of the flow of energy that constituted the activities of the members and staff of Parliament and the government, then the addition of new actors would increase the flow of energy that constituted the government. The addition of actors also implies the addition of energy in the form of travel, handling of papers, and so on. The flow, therefore, that was the government and the flow that was Parliament were increasing by the addition of new elements; and these elements simultaneously brought about changes in the structures of these organizations.

Until a few years ago, it was practically impossible to speak of the processes of energy flow in any way that was useful for the study of human society outside of a strictly ecological analysis that simply took the human component as one part of the animal community. This changed with the work of Prigogine (1967; see also Prigogine, Allen, and Herman 1977) and the delineation of *dissipative structures* as a part of the physical world. Life does follow the laws of classical dynamics and thermodynamics, but not in any simple and direct manner. Indeed, it used to be argued that the second law of thermodynamics was contradicted by the life processes, because the former described only breakdown, whereas the latter clearly described an increase in complexity.

Dissipative structures exist under conditions that are very *far from equilibrium*. They are *input–output systems* wherein the system or structure itself is composed of the content of the input. Thus all life forms are kinds of dissipative structures. Let us take as an example the oyster. During its period of growth, the oyster feeds on nutrients in the sea and converts these into shell and into the animal itself. The growing oyster is literally composed of the conversion of nutrients and the dissipation of their energy. As such, *it is the process of dissipation that constitutes the structure*. When the oyster – the animal – is separated from the shell, both the oyster and the shell cease to grow. They cannot take in any more energy or matter, and they cease to comprise a dissipative structure. The shell may dissipate, but it can never again grow; it can only decline, wear away, or break up. All forms of life are constituted by continuing energetic inputs, such complex sets of energy forms as oxygen, biochemicals, and minerals. Thus dissipative structures are different from other structures – such as the oyster shell or the house – in that it is the constant consumption of the energetic inputs that comprise the structure. Dissipative structures are potentially unstable, because they cannot exist long and will disintegrate if the inputs cease to flow. Thus a dissipative structure is composed of constantly changing flow that succeeds in maintaining a particular form by maintaining a particular input.

The argument that lies behind the present study is that *societies operate as dissipative structures;* they are continuities of form that are constituted by the very flow of energy that is expended (i.e., converted) in the process of acting out the behaviors and doing the work (from both human and nonhuman sources) that is carried on in the context of social relationships. In the language of earlier work on energy in society, the expression "harnessing energy" has been used (White 1943). This is somewhat misleading in the present context because it implies a subject–object distinction between society and the energy it uses, as with, for instance, the automobile and the gasoline it uses. In dissipative structures, however, subject and object are one. Society is composed of the energy it consumes; hence, it can be treated as a dissipative structure.

Organized aggregates of human beings, then, operate as dissipative structures and, as such, have some special characteristics that are common to such structures but differ in at least one important feature. They are alike in that:

1. They are in constant *fluctuation*. One aspect of their being far from equilibrium is that they are subject to many irregularities both within

their own complex structure and from *perturbations* in the environment. No measure of their activity can therefore be expected to be very constant.

2. Their historical course traces a stochastic path, subject to changes that are essentially unpredictable before the conjunction of circumstances that causes them. This means that there is an essential indeterminism involved in certain phases of their behavior.

3. In the course of their histories, they come to bifurcation points, situations in which their future history might go in one direction or another. At these times, indeterministic elements may decide a move in one way or another.

4. In societies, a major change has to do with continuing expansion. When expanding, they reach points where the particular internal arrangements no longer suffice to handle the amount and kinds of energy flow that constitute them. These are bifurcation points. A social structure may move on to greater expansion, to dissolution, to decline, or may remain in a fluctuating *steady state,* that is, where input and output remain essentially equal.

Societies differ from other kinds of dissipative structures in the achievement of a steady state. Prigogine, in his delineation of dissipative structures in physical chemistry, regarded the presence of a steady state to be an identifying characteristic. Societies, however, share the expansion-for-survival that characterizes all life. A society achieves a steady state when there is some restriction on inputs that inhibits a continuing expansion. It is likely that such constrictions on inputs can finally be traced to environmental limitations. But in the interplay that constitutes living, it is often difficult to fix the "origin" of a chain of events, and the internal complexity of such structures can contrive many devices that act as triggers over inputs or that inhibit the useful internal funneling of flows. There is no question that human societies have achieved steady states. Well-adapted foraging societies are among the prime examples. While the evidence is far from adequate, my impression from the scattered cases available is that most such societal steady states stem ultimately from the recognition of real environmental limitations to the known abilities of the society, or from an effective combination of triggers to population expansion in which the energetic quality of the processes may be relatively little understood. What is perhaps most important to stress at this point, however, is that there is nothing universally inherent in social organizations that leads to a steady state.

In complex societies, the problem of the steady state is very important; as mentioned earlier, it was the manifestation of a kind of steady state in Great Britain between 1910 and 1950 revealed in the Humphrey and Stanislaw (1979) study that drew my attention to the material that constitutes this monograph. The growth of population that marked the preceding centuries, and the growth of energy use per capita that resulted from the industrial revolution and the world trade that accompanied it, were expansions of striking proportions. They were made possible by the conjunction of many economic, biomedical, technological, and social relational elements. Much of what composed them has gone under the general rubric of "capitalism," and in that sense the term stands for a great, complex *catalytic mechanism* that releases flows of energy for expansion. But why did Great Britain move into a steady state when it did, and why did it remain so for the time it did? This study addresses the first of these questions.

The governing or regulation of societies as dissipative structures brings us back to the subject of triggers. The energy forms and flows that conjoin to constitute dissipative structures become in one way or another self-regulating. One way of conceiving of this is to differentiate certain energetic flows (usually microflows, but not exclusively so) that have specific regulative tasks. Hierarchy theorists (Pattee 1973) have called these *descriptive* processes, as in the operation of the gene. They carry the *plans* or *templates* that direct growth and certain behaviors, as well as the *regulatory mechanisms* that respond to environmental perturbations. Thus whether a given dissipative structure is in a steady state depends on the actions of regulative mechanisms that may themselves be dissipative structures.

Britain pioneered in some regulatory triggers that facilitated the flow of energy in important ways in the nineteenth century. Although Marconi invented his telegraph in Italy, it was in Great Britain that he was able to put it into extensive service. The penny post, a British invention, had a profound effect on world communications, and the British similarly led in the establishment of the International Postal Agreements. Indeed, the very bankruptcies and institutional failures that dotted late-nineteenth-century history provided the experience that was put to work by insurance firms such as Lloyds. (I am indebted to Nicolas Barker for calling these cases to my attention.)

Why did not the government, a major regulative element in the British state, act to trigger the release of more energy back into Great Britain rather than allowing such triggers to be sent overseas? I suggest in Chapter 8 that the regulative mechanism was not adequately developed to exercise or extend such power over the multitude of decision-making centers that are contained within the British system. The decisions of most investors and companies were not centralized as parts of great conglomerates, and the power centralized in the nation-state could be extended just so far at the time. Also, other decision-making centers, such as labor unions and extraparliamentary interest groups, offered further competition at the same time.

An additional characteristic of social dissipative structures concerns *boundaries*. Social organization and societies are lightly integrated, what H. Simon (1969:73–4) calls decomposable; the tightness of the interdependence of the parts varies greatly. In comparison with the organism, for example, the nexus of relating processes in society is not as tightly or as functionally integrated. A society can disintegrate, but many of its parts will continue to survive as operative dissipative structures. The important regulative events in society depend on symbols that are subject to noise and misreading. This is much less so of organisms. If my arm misreads my brain's instructions, we call it pathology. In society, misreading happens all the time and we accept it as a normal, if irritating, part of the procedure.

Societal parts may find (or invent, or happen upon) a new arrangement that permits them to take different forms, to redefine themselves. Essentially this happens when an expanding structure reaches a level of operation in which its internal parts can no longer handle the amount and kind of energy taken in. To continue to expand, new mechanisms must come into being, the parts must be somewhat rearranged, and a new and (in this case) larger structure must emerge. While the result is clearly a continuity deriving from the earlier structure, there is also a new structure, different from its predecessor especially in size and regulation. The points at which such profound integrative changes are made are the bifurcation points mentioned earlier. Nothing says that the appropriate regulative devices *have* to come into being, because it is quite possible at such times that the ecology is constricting the society's growth. It is also possible that the existing regulative mechanisms are damaged by the expansion, and in the absence of a new or better one, the structure simply begins to decompose.

A question that arises from the work of the economic historians on which this study is based, but that cannot be fully answered here, is why the internal structure of Great Britain acted as it did during the last third of the nineteenth century. It is a working assumption that the decisions made were rational from the points of view of the decision makers; but it is equally recognized that this explains very little. The increasing flow of energy generated by the growing industrial system brought in its train a set of new social emergences – in organizations of the working population, of entrepreneurs, of engineers, and so forth. Although I have made no attempt here to measure the amount of energy that was triggered abroad by the overseas investment of money and skills, it seems reasonable to assume that a greater internal investment would also have yielded some increased flow at home. To the inhabitants of the country at the time, however, the answer was apparently fairly clear.

I have described most of this as if it were largely the result of chance. Of course, human societies have cultures that are dedicated in part to trying to assure that the inputs are kept up and that adjustments are made when necessary. Culture itself is a very important and complex set of regulatory mechanisms, devices that emerged in the course of evolution that have given the human species a particular finite advantage over many other competing species. The core mechanism of culture is the arbitrary assignation of meanings to energetic forms. This predominantly human psychological process is intrinsically an expansive one, because it acts through trial and error to enhance the energetic flows of the world. Like life itself, culture is an expansive catalytic agent, a series of regulatory devices that will tend to expand energy flows unless specifically programmed otherwise. The nature of the well-adapted culture poses conservative features against progressive features, because both are useful adaptive devices at different times. For a culture to be consistently expansive or conservative would probably be maladaptive in the long run. It is the flexibility offered by the two strategies that provides the advantage.

A central principle to the operation of dissipative structures in nature is *Lotka's principle:*

In every instance considered, natural selection will so operate as to increase the total mass of the organic system, to increase the rate of circulation of matter through the system, and to increase the total energy flux through the system so long as there is presented an unutilized residue of matter and available energy. [Lotka 1922:148]

Lotka formulated this principle many years before the notion of dissipative structure was available. He wrote in terms of flows, of energy flux and matter. The argument made earlier about the relation between flow and structure, however, obviously fits within the assertions made by Lotka. Dissipative structures illustrate the advantages of increasing the energy flux, and competition between them constitutes a natural part of the process. Social dissipative structures are such that one is composed of many others, and the parts of one structure may simultaneously compose parts of another. Thus it is that societies can expand; for they are composed of many emerging subunits, interlocking and interdependent in different degrees of integration and hierarchization.

Certainly a proper study of Great Britain in this era would require attention to the emerging social elements in the society. I have elsewhere (Adams 1981, in preparation) endeavored to set forth a framework for such a study, but the task of analyzing the vast material on British society of this era is far beyond me at

the moment. Nevertheless, a proper study of the history of the relationship between energy flow and the society that it composes would require that we try to
detail the various emerging sectors, to estimate the amount of energy that they
cost and that they produced, and to postulate how they related to each other.

By using the concept of the dissipative structure in conjunction with Lotka's
principle, we can see how a given social structure might simultaneously (1) try
to increase the circulation of energy through itself and (2) use its own output to
increase circulation through a larger structure that constitutes a part of its environment in order to assure itself of future inputs. It is a well-recognized ecological principle that an organism or a population of organisms evolves as a part of
its environment, and not independently of it. Thus the notion that a given society
must simultaneously see to its own inputs and to the flows that will sustain its
environment is in no sense novel.

This process of simultaneously feeding itself and feeding the environment is
central to the analyses of Great Britain in this study. We have no deterministic
rule that says that any society has to survive forever, and the history of humanity
suggests that most do not, at least not in any integrated continuity. Just as the
gene is argued to contribute to the reproduction of itself, it may be argued that
the principal evolutionary role of a society is to contribute to future societies.
There is a problem, however, in applying this sociobiological assertion to society. The British case suggests that societies have a role in creating and sustaining
other societies as well as creating their own more direct successors. Social reproduction, in this light, becomes more than the process of reiterating contemporary
social forms. It inherently implies expansion and diversification, and the loss of
the individuality of the producing society.

Selection explanations

An adequate explanatory model based on the evolutionary framework has to
account for both a variation-producing component and a selective component.
There is no reason to expect, however, that all aspects of scientific activity proceed at the same pace; and in biological evolution it is generally accepted that
the understanding of mutation is far less satisfactory than is that of selection.
Selective factors operate in the relative light of day, whereas mutative processes
are still deep within the genetic phase.

Explaining complex phenomena is a problem of a different order than is that
of simple processes. The kinds of explanations that sufficed for classical or New-
tonian dynamics obviously cannot cope with the nonlinear processes characteristic of living organisms. Nevertheless, there has persisted in our framework of
explanation for living and social processes an inherent plan or strategy that is

derived from the logic of explanation of such classical processes. In explaining events, we tend to seek what is essentially a combination of Aristotelian efficient and material causes, the antecedent conditions that are asserted to be responsible for generating the event in question. Even in simple cases, however, it has long been obvious that such statements about known antecedents are seldom adequate. Thus, to explain the cause of a person getting up and moving from one room to another, we must identify the psychological, physiological, and environmental factors that operate in a most complex interaction quite beyond anything more than the crudest kinds of specification. Nevertheless, there is a tendency in social science to persist in seeking these kinds of causal explanations.

In the search for reasons behind complex social events, we do sometimes resort to a very different kind of explanation. Compare the following ways of characterizing the "cause" of the presence of communities among human beings: (1) human beings live in communities because they are gregarious; (2) human beings live in communities because they are interdependent. The first statement asserts that there are antecedent conditions in human beings that will lead them to seek to form communities with other human beings. The second statement asserts that if human beings failed to live in communities, then they could not survive economically or genetically. This second explanation has often been interpreted as being couched in terms of final causes, an Aristotelian variety that is widely rejected by serious science.

In recent decades, however, the second explanation has been seen in another light and is perhaps best illustrated by its legitimation in biology as an evolutionary explanation. (See Skinner [1981] for a recent exposition.) Various terms have been used to differentiate this kind of explanation from the first. The old and the new have been characterized respectively as (1) "proximate" and (2) "ultimate"; (1) "functional" and (2) "evolutionary"; (1) the "how?" and (2) the "why?"; (1) the "mechanism" and (2) the "strategy"; and (1) in terms of the "immediate environmental factors" and (2) in terms of the "long-term consistent pattern of environmental change" (Pianka 1978:15; see also Baker 1938, Mayr 1961, and E. O. Wilson 1975:23). Pianka argues that the difference between the two "is in outlook, between thinking in an 'ecological' time scale (now time) or in an 'evolutionary' time scale (geological time)" (1978:15). The term "ultimate" is applied to the second because it refers to the fact that antecedent genetic characteristics continue to make themselves felt over long eras, in contrast to the more immediate or "proximate" factors that can be seen to operate in a given case.

It is not with any desire to muddy the waters with additional terminology that leads me to prefer yet another term for this second kind of explanation: *selection explanation*. Rather, the fundamental characteristic involved is that it argues that some events are the product of natural selection. Because natural selection usually takes a long time – and in the world of genetic biology, it clearly takes a long time – the time element may appear to be of major importance. But I would suggest that the time element is relative. What makes this kind of explanation different from the other is the process of selection, not how long it takes. Moreover, the use of this term suggests further aspects of the process that perhaps have not been emphasized sufficiently in the work of the biologists. First, the events being explained are extremely complex, comprising factors that are ancient – as is the pattern of a gene – and factors that are much more recent – such as a forest fire that may kill the remaining members of a small genetic population. Such an explanation does not pretend to search for and list all the historical events that finally contribute to the presence of a given form. It merely asserts that the form is the product of a series of events that are often too complex to ascertain. This does not block the postulation of a proximate model of how it occurred; but such a model usually has its share of estimates and imprecisions, and is also necessarily incomplete.

Closely related to this characteristic of complexity is that explanations couched in terms of selection contribute to prediction only under stable conditions. They are inherently ex post facto explanations for some specific historical outcome of a long and complex selection process. There is seldom any reason to anticipate that a given selection process will be repeated precisely. But to the degree that an explanation based on selection denotes a specific set of factors that operate in other situations, they can be used as the basis for a hypothesis to predict some class of events. To return to our original example of the community, it is a prediction (although an obvious one) that those human beings who fail to participate in a community will have a very low probability of reproducing subsequent generations.

If selection explanations are so limited in the kinds of predictions they permit, what value do they have? The answer to this must vary with the particular problems and fields of investigation. Pianka points out that the two ways of explanation are not mutually exclusive. Ecological and physiological mechanisms evolve in response to evolutionary and environmental conditions (Pianka 1978). E. O. Wilson is actually less sympathetic to the "proximate" arguments, holding that they tend to be phrased in "nebulous independent variables" that "can seldom be linked either to neurophysiology or evolutionary biology and hence to the remainder of science" (1975:23).

In the present context, the importance of selection explanations rests on a somewhat different basis. Where we deal with aggregates of antecedents that are too complex, too multitudinous, and/or too little known to sort out, we are left with no choice but to resort to selection explanations. Thus the proximate "causes" of the relative deceleration of energy consumption and of the asserted "decline" of Britain in the late nineteenth century are by far too complicated and too little known to ever unravel in a way suitable to even a random minority of historians. Instead, we must resort to an explanation based on selection.

Selection explanations are particularly useful for examining novel historical events. Since every such event is unique, an attempt to seek an explanation requires that we explore a diverse range of factors that played a conjunctive role in the final event. While it may be occasionally possible to account for the course of history with a few factors, for larger and more complex events we can at best have recourse only to selection explanations. For example, one can argue that the discovery of analogies in comparative history will provide a kind of explanation (cf. Stinchcombe 1978), but such analogies are actually statements that similar outcomes seem to have evolved from similar sets of conditions, suggesting that there may be patterns of selection that can be delineated.

Given this perspective on the nature of the explanation of complex events, we can reflect again on the usages of the biologists and ecologists cited earlier. Their terms ("proximate," "functional," "mechanical," and "immediate environmental factors") describe an explanation that concerns the variation-producing phase of events, that is, innovation, mutation, and the appearance of the novel. The inadequacies of proximate explanations that led Wilson to discount them in favor of ultimate explanations thus stems from the fact that a satisfactory proximate explanation would have to describe how a mutation occurred; and it is precisely this that biology finds most difficult. I would extend this, however, and argue that the study of culture and society finds it equally difficult to predict the appearance of *new* things. Once invented, it is much less difficult to suggest that something will be replicated, reinvented or destroyed. But before it is invented the first time, we have no way of foreseeing what may occur. Hence, I would argue that "ultimate" or selective explanations must play a central role in social science studies as well as biological studies for elucidating the process of natural selection for the very reason that we may never have adequate proximate explanations.

The role of energy in social process has many aspects, one being that it constricts or inhibits action. Knowing the amount of energy available may not provide a good predictive tool for saying how it will be used, but it is a very strong indicator of what the limits of activity may be. Knowing the amount of fuel in a vehicle will not predict whether a trip will be started, but upon embarkation, it will certainly give some indication of how far the vehicle will go. Thus energy provides the basis for a selection explanation wherever the energy cost of a given activity is known. Any theory that gives us a better understanding of how energy costs operate therefore provides an analytical tool for understanding process on the basis of selection.

A summary of some assumptions

There lurks behind every inquiry into past failures a visceral hope that something will have relevance for our current and future problems. Contemporary inquiries always bring knowledge of events subsequent to those investigated and often pose questions that never occurred to the actors of the time. There is no way that we can ever really see things through their eyes, particularly the diversified, collective view of people of vastly different economic and social circumstances. Efforts to do so always result in controversial assertions that reflect as much about the advocates as they do about the events being considered.

My study cannot evade the time and place of its own birth. I propose to work in terms of certain assumptions that focus attention on certain aspects of these earlier processes. They are as follows:

1. I assume that everyone generally acts rationally; that is, people make decisions whenever possible that will be to their own best interests as they perceive them. Thus if certain events take a direction that seems illogical or exotic, we first assume that it is our view that is illogical and unfamiliar and that the actors had some idea about what they were doing that is perhaps not clear to us. Insofar as we want to phrase ideas in terms of human motivation, our job is not to take them to task for irrationality but to construct a line of reason that makes sense in terms of the times and that might at least be coherent with what they did. To assume that everyone "generally acts rationally" is not to assert that everyone really does. Too often people do not see all the relevant factors they should consider, or they are incapable of carrying out the logical process that rational decision making requires, or they may simply be too tired to make the effort. Events too often are acted out in terms of other factors, and the decisions made turn out to be very minor, often contrary parts of the larger process.

An obvious concomitant to this assumption about rationalism is that we equally assume that decisions made by individuals concern us, not merely the conjunction of processes beyond the control of human beings. Only *thinking individuals* – and both terms here are equally important – can act rationally.

Because the identification of motives is always hypothetical and can rarely be confirmed, it is never possible to construct a history composed of the motives that may have preceded or accompanied the actions that took place. Occasionally, we can establish motives with some reasonable certainty; more often, however, we have little knowledge of what went on in the nervous systems of the actors. Time spent in identifying motives may in some sense provide confirmation of a model that we are making of some historical process. But it is equally the construction of an illusion that allows us to think we are seeing things through the eyes of the actors; it tries to satisfy the investigator's egotism in the search for coherence in the materials. What we must do is seek other rules to guide us.

2. I assume that history follows a stochastic path, but the course of the evolution of the human species suggests that there is some order in the residue of natural selection. Whereas the course of history of any given social grouping or society is fairly unpredictable apart from periods of particular stability, the overall course of general evolution (in the sense that Sahlins [1960] uses the term) has been to favor societies that were able to control greater amounts of energy, providing resources were available. This is essentially Lotka's (1922) principle. Given that it is a selection explanation, however, it does provide low predictability for any particular case, since the immediate strategies are more important in particular cases. Thus the order that we seek is one of selective processes.

3. Every event in history can occur only insofar as there is available whatever amount of energy (i.e., work) is necessary to carry it out. We can think thoughts wildly, but if we do not have the wherewithal to convert them into action, they will remain thoughts. There are two fundamental phases of energetic activity that must be present in every event. The first is the flow of energy, obtained by altering the relationship between a given form and its environment. This is the major activity (or activities) that identifies the event. In addition, however, there must also be the regulatory actions that trigger the substantive flow. Events are thus composed of the related action of triggers and released flows. In seeking energetic priorities, we are concerned with the structure of the event, not its history. History acts in unpredictable ways. Events in history, however, necessarily take on a structure or organization that must accord with their energetic components. Thus this study starts with the course of energy expenditure in the United Kingdom, not because I believe that it will provide "an explanation" but because it is the substantive product of natural selective processes. I seek to find out how the processes of rationalism, randomness, and energy costs worked conjunctively as selective mechanisms.

4. A cardinal characteristic of life is that it is an expanding process. The study of evolution maps this process in terms of time, place, and content. The theory of evolution proposes the major outlines of the process – mutation, replication or reproduction, and natural selection. But in all this, we assume that life is an expansive process, or else none of the other theoretical components would have a place. The same assumption must be made for human development. The normal process of human life is expansive. The differentiation made between population evolution and cultural evolution is an academic one made on the basis that it takes different kinds of tools to study these different facets of human expansion. In fact, cultural expansion is merely an extension of biological expansion, and to see it in any other way leads one quickly to confusion, which is unfortunately too common in the literature.

This is not to say that all human populations and societies are expanding at all times. Most life operates in complex environments, and there are ample selection processes that constantly challenge the expansive surges, slowing them, often inhibiting them, and even destroying them. Thus the study of history is in part the study of the search for the way to expand, because expansion is the only way that history and genetics teach us that survival occurs. Evolution, however, is not only the course of that expansion but also its constrictions and failure.

As a strategy of research, it may be argued that explanations in human history should pay more attention to the processes of inhibition. In a sense, mutation and invention and discovery will take place from time to time whether we understand them or not. Further understanding might provide a greater control over them, but if the history of culture and of capitalism teaches us anything, it teaches us that the success of expansive inventions is manifested in their becoming self-reproductive, self-expanding. The real controls, the regulation and triggers that nature exercises over expansion, are realized through inhibitions. The human species, as a part of this natural selective process, can operate more effectively if it can handle the processes of inhibition. In a fuller sense, the study of history is the study of the workings of natural selection on the efforts of the human species to expand; hence, natural selection is a most important area of study.

Thus far the human species has expanded in accord with the first portion of Lotka's principle. But there is the final clause: "so long as there is presented an unutilized residue of matter and available energy." This is the reminder that there is a fundamental and ultimate inhibitor to expansion: the scarcity of energetic materials to sustain it.

5. The term "natural selection" is used in this monograph to refer to the entire set of substantive processes and events that affect the course of other events. Natural selection is not some monolith that comes crashing down on the dreams and desires of human beings. Rather, it is the conjunction (often fragmented and in no sense organized) of obstacles and inhibitions, both large and small, that nature and man collectively bring together to divert and sometimes direct the course of history. A "selection explanation" is one that attempts to recognize these conjunctions and then to ascertain and detail their component parts and dynamics. Human beings are not merely confronted by natural selection, but their behavior comprises an ongoing part of the process. Human conflict and human cooperation are equally part of the selective process, just as are the amount of energy available from the sun, the amount of food produced with a given amount of water, and the amount of returns on a foreign investment.

3. The leveling off of energy consumption

It is clear that serious observers of the late Victorian era recognized that British "decline" was not absolute but, rather, relative. The problem in both assertions, however, was to identify the nature of the decline in something more than the visceral feelings of threatened businessmen or itchy imperialists. The hardest figures available had principally to do with the relative growth of industry and business in the United Kingdom as compared with that of Germany and the United States. These certainly were telling matters, but not all British industry and commerce were suffering, and many sectors of the population continued to see general benefits arising from the larger process. Indeed, for those whose guiding light was the growth of national income, the per capita rate of increase generally was little affected by these matters until the turn of the century (see Figure 3.4).

Nevertheless, something of considerable importance was "declining" during this late Victorian era: the growth of per capita energy consumption. Humphrey and Stanislaw (1979) have shown that between 1870 and 1910, the per capita energy consumption growth curve leveled off (Figure 3.1). The level then reached was generally maintained until about 1950, when growth renewed as part of the larger world increase in petroleum use. We do not have yearly figures for energy use before 1910, but those from that year make it clear that the phenomenon was one of continuing fluctuation, extremely sensitive to current events, reflecting the increase in use during the two world wars and the declines of the periods of strikes and depressions. Figure 3.2 shows the overall commercial energy and coal consumption as well as the per capita coal consumption for that period.

If we are to discuss some kind of "state" of the British system in this era, certainly the quantity of energy consumed is as good an indication of the general condition as any single measure we could find. It would make itself felt in diverse ways in many aspects of the society. Note that we are concerned with energy consumption, not energy production. Coal, the major source of commercial energy, continued to be produced in an increasing amount (Figure 3.3), with only temporary declines, until World War I. There was a significant growth in the export of coal, however, beginning in the second half of the century, and this

29

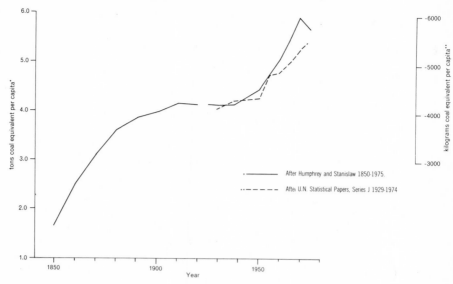

Figure 3.1. U.K. energy consumption per capita, 1850–1972. (Note: Five-year intervals for Humphrey and Stanislaw data and for U.N. data after 1950; prior U.N. data are for 1929 and 1937 only.)

was the principal material factor in the relative decline in the general energy consumption figures.

In energy terms, then, Great Britain entered a steady state just before World War I, a condition in which it was, on the average, producing no more energy on a per capita basis than it was consuming. While there are violent fluctuations, rising by as much as 0.8 ton coal equivalent per capita (tce/capita) during the two world wars, and dropping as much as one tce/capita during the major strikes of the depression in the 1920s and 1930s, fuel consumption returned to a level between 4.0 and 4.3 tce/capita after each major fluctuation through the end of World War II. After this, the irregular rise of the third quarter of the century began.

Figure 3.4 suggests the relation of this fuel and energy history to that of the growth of national income. There is nothing in the behavior of the national income growth before 1900 to suggest that there is any secular change in overall energy consumption in the country except a brief decline in the 1870s and 1890s, and then the leveling off at the end of the century. On the other hand, the sharp recovery of energy consumption beginning in 1932–3 is paralleled in the income figures. Thus the energy figures give a somewhat different picture of the course of events than do the national income figures. First, the former clearly indicate a serious leveling off beginning in the 1870s, whereas the latter do not consistently reflect this until the turn of the century. Second, the recovery from the ''depths'' of the depression is more graphically visible in the energy figures than in the income figures, since the latter seem to start from a much higher level than do the former. It is important, I believe, that the energy per capita figures better reflect a map of general feeling of the times than do the national income figures.

There are three issues that need to be mentioned here. First is that by the second quarter of this century, coal served less and less as an index of energy costs, in Britain or anywhere else (see Figure 3.2A). Coal was already an important fuel in domestic and manufacturing activities by the beginning of the nineteenth century. Its early growth, however, resulted from the growth of the iron industry, the steam engine, and, late in the century, the export market. In the larger picture, ''fuel'' was diversifying. Coal alone was a sufficient measure in the late nineteenth century, but by the 1920s there was a noticeable increment of other energy sources. In the depths of the 1930s' depression, other energy sources constituted 5% of the total, and by the end of the war they reached almost 9%. The subsequent rise was gradual until 1956, when coal began a sharp absolute decline. From 1930 on, then, we must exercise more caution in dealing with different commercial energy sources; in the post–World War II years, the relative proportions changed radically as Britain fully entered the petroleum period.

The second issue is energy efficiency. Our figures concern absolute fuel consumption. If we look at British society as a large dissipative structure, fuel consumption constitutes one of the principal inputs to that society. What happens then, however, is a much more complicated issue. Fuel was most readily used for its heat, an appropriate use. The ''work'' yielded by this expenditure of heat varied, of course, with many factors. Thus the efficiency of the conversion is a very important variable. Stoves are usually more efficient than open fires, and some stoves are more efficient than others; what is accomplished with a given amount of input of fuel increases with systematic technological improvements. Between the late nineteenth century and 1950, there was unquestionably a notable increase in the efficiency of certain kinds of conversions.

In the generation of electricity, the efficiency in the United Kingdom increased from 8% in 1900 to an average of 25% in the 1970s, today, with a ''best efficiency'' of close to 40%. Chapman (1975), however, points out how the improved efficiency may be more than offset by increasing energy costs of conversion. The increasing difficulty of obtaining energy raw materials (more accessible, poorer-grade ores are more technically difficult to extract) raises precipitously the amounts of energy necessary (i.e., the energy cost) for extraction and con-

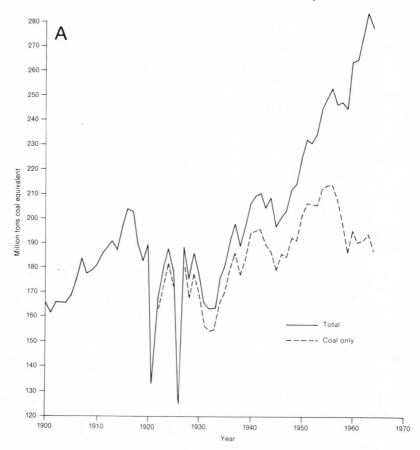

Figure 3.2. *A:* U.K. domestic fuel consumption, 1900–64. (*Source:* London and Cambridge Economic Service, *The British Economy: Key Statistics 1900–1964.*) *B:* U.K. domestic fuel consumption per capita, 1900–64. (*Sources:* London and Cambridge Economic Service 1967; dated entries from Humphrey and Stanislaw 1979; 1968 and 1972 data from Darmstedter, Dunkerly, and Alterman 1977.)

version, thus neutralizing the simple improvements in direct conversion (Chapman 1975:89–90). The conversion of coal to electricity is not the end of the story; how will the electricity be used? If it is used directly for running a motor, which is an appropriate use, then the efficiency can presumably be seen as a gain. If it is used in inappropriate ways, however, such as heating, then it may constitute a loss. Chapman shows that for the United Kingdom, between 1950

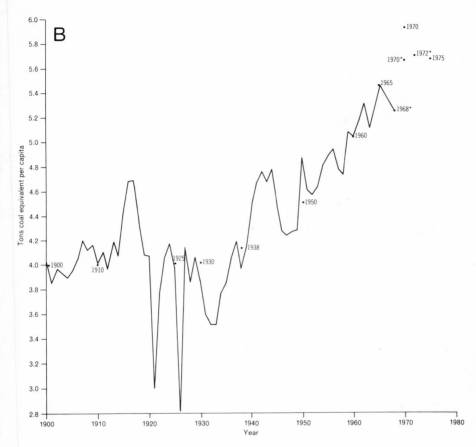

and 1970, the amount of heat delivered to domestic users leveled off just above 400×10^9 kWh; during this same period, however, the primary fuel required to yield this consumer utilization had increased sharply from 500×10^9 kWh to well over 700×10^9 kWh (Chapman 1975:129). Given these considerations for all fuel industries, Chapman argues that the overall efficiency of the fuel industries between 1950 and 1972 declined from approximately 87% to 68%.

Further research on changes in efficiency in the late nineteenth century is unquestionably important here. The data are not very extensive. There are ample indications that there were some changes, in iron and steel and in coke. Humphrey and Stanislaw say that the efficiency in pig iron use of coal between 1870 and 1914 was such that whereas ''about 3 tons of coal were required to produce

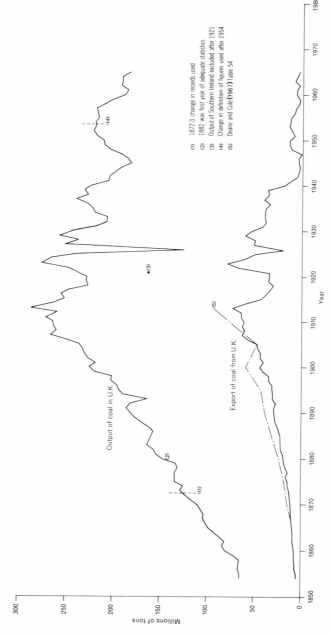

Figure 3.3. Outputs and exports of coal, United Kingdom, 1854–1965. (*Sources*: 1854 to 1938 from Mitchell and Deane 1962; 1938 to 1965 from Mitchell and Jones 1971.)

The following labels appear within the figure:

Millions of tons

Output of coal in U.K.

Export of coal from U.K.

Year

(1) 1872-3 change in records used
(2) 1882 was first year of adequate statistics
(3) Output of Southern Ireland excluded after 1921
(4) Change in definition of figures used after 1954
(5) Deane and Cole (1967) Table 54

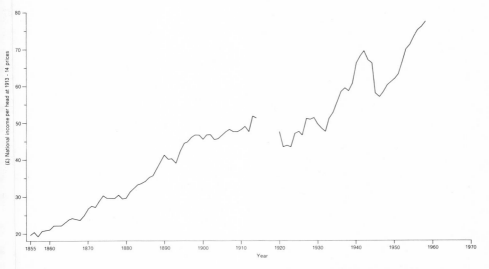

Figure 3.4. United Kingdom: growth of national income per head at 1913–14 prices, 1855–1959. (After Deane and Cole 1967: Table 90; deflated by retail price index.)

1 ton of pig iron in 1870, the amount required had fallen to about 2 tons by 1914'' (1979:49). Similar improvements in efficiency might be claimed for other industries. Putnam suggests that the general increase in efficiency from 1860 to 1900 was from 8% to 10% (1953:90). In general, we must allow that there was an increase in efficiency in some industries and that this would have been re-flected in their output. On the other hand, the increase in energy costs of extrac-tion and conversions should also presumably be allowed for. At present, there seems to be no sure way of achieving adequate estimates on these questions.

The third issue is whether the reduction of consumption of coal was in any sense the result of a shortage or reduction in availability. The answer seems to be no. The rate of growth of coal production dropped between 1875 and 1885 (see Figure 3.3), but the absolute production continued to expand until 1913. There were slight dips in the 1870s and 1880s, but until the turn of the century these constituted only slight fluctuations in what was predominantly a steady progression.

In 1865, W. Stanley Jevons published what in retrospect is a fascinating study of British coal production and use. He knew that coal was the basic motivating force of contemporary civilization and that Britain had a very large amount of good coal; but he feared that its supply would be depleted. Because, from the perspective of the time, coal appeared to be the only motivating power for in-

Table 3.1. *Jevons's estimates of future coal consumption for*
Great Britain compared with actual coal production (in
millions of long tons)

Year	Consumption Jevons's assumed rate of increase	Production
1861	83.6	86.3
1871	117.9	121.2
1881	166.3	159.2
1891	234.7	191.5
1901	331.0	226.1
1911	466.9	280.7
1921	658.6	168.5
1931	929.0	226.5[a]
1941	1,310.5	213.0
1951	1,848.6	229.4
1961	2,607.5	196.7

[a] Southern Ireland excluded beginning at this date.
Source: Jevons (1865:213); Mitchell (1975:Table D2).

dustry, Jevons's fear was not illogical. On the basis of what seem to be reasonably sound estimates, he calculated that the growth of coal consumption in Great Britain during the era immediately before 1863 was 3.5% per year. Projecting this, he produced the figures in Table 3.1. His figures are close for the first two decades predicted. Thereafter the increase of the estimate departs increasingly from the real production. Jevons seems not to have differentiated between coal production and consumption, and thus his figures are probably higher than they should be for the latter. He did note that there was a significant export of coal, but he did not address the question of further export increases. He was concerned with whether Great Britain would eventually have to import coal but concluded it was impossible, because the growth of imports over exports was mainly in products that took coal to manufacture; and to export coal only to use it to produce other coal for import obviously was not reasonable.

Aside from the estimates and fears expressed by Jevons, his very concern for the coal reserves is especially interesting. His cry was heeded even less in the Great Britain of the 1860s than is the cry of oil conservationists in the United States today. While he was not particularly farsighted, his concern was well taken. What did happen was that production did not follow the rate he projected that it might; rather, the reserves became more difficult to mine and the growth of production declined. Total production did continue to increase, however, until it was sharply affected by the war.

The most likely reason behind such an unexciting performance would be a lack of market. But this does not seem to have been the case. The price did fall during much of the 1870s and 1880s, but the period 1890–1914 was one of general prosperity with only occasional difficult years (Taylor 1968:13). This prosperity seemed to rest on certain advantages that Britain held in the export market. Even though by the first part of the twentieth century Britain paid higher wages than did continental mines, it had greater labor productivity, and many of its mines were located near the sea, thus facilitating overseas shipments. These advantages were negated by the war, but they were sufficient to lead to the impressive spurt during the years immediately preceding the conflict.

Labor productivity in coal mines hit a high during the 1860s. It dropped from more than 300 tons per worker per year in the 1870s but rose again for the decade 1880–90. It then underwent a fluctuating decline that, in 1913, reached a low of 239 tons per worker per year, constituting a reduction of some 20%. The causes of this decline seem to have been a combination of factors, most of which were interdependent and related to the improved situation for the miners. Brown and Browne (1968) have reviewed this problem in some depth and argue that a reduction in working hours was broadly responsible for some of the apparent productivity decline per man-year. With this was an unmistakable change in the attitudes of the people, signaled by the rise of a more militant unionism. They argue also that employers in the United Kingdom were less resistant to unionism than were employers in the United States. Attitudes changed from "a fair day's wage for a fair day's work" to a competitive attitude for higher wages for increased consumption (Brown and Browne 1968:184–6).

An additional factor that affected older mines more than the new was that British coal reserves had been under exploration for over 400 years and were wearing thin. Coal was harder to get out. In view of this, it seems likely that a sensitive industry would take advantage of the technological and organizational opportunities that were becoming available during this era. The U.K. coal industry generally did not. Coal cut by machine seriously began only in 1900 and did not affect more than 10% of the production before the war (Mitchell and Deane 1962:123). Concern with this was not hidden. Criticisms were published in 1902 arguing that in the United States, 20% of coal output (which was some 240 million tons) was machine-cut, whereas almost none was machine-cut in Britain (Taylor 1968:56). Germany's coal production modernized much more rapidly than did Britain's, and by 1913 it had nearly caught up with the British level of production (Henderson 1975:235).

Efforts at organizational efficiency were also turned aside by the mine owners. The industry was composed of more than 3,000 separate collieries in more than 1,500 separate businesses. Of these, 118 collieries produced a quarter of the total coal output, and each had more than 2,000 workers (Taylor 1968:63). Efforts to form either national- or regional-level trusts in the 1890s, to reduce competition and in general rationalize the industry, were firmly resisted (Taylor 1968:65).

Was British consumption of coal limited by lack of coal, or by something else? Would greater production of coal have led to greater use of coal in the United Kingdom, or could more production have stimulated greater consumption? The answer, again, seems to be that consumption varied independently of production. In Figure 3.3 and in Table 3.2 it is clear that there was an increase in coal production far beyond domestic demands; indeed, the increasing foreign market was probably the major stimulus to the increased production of the early twentieth century. The use to which the growing coal production was put is revealing (see Table 3.2). Between 1869 and 1913, total coal production increased from 110.7 to 310.9 million tons, or an increase of 180.8%. The increase in coal used in Great Britain was only 120.7% in this period. Domestic household consumption increased by 89.2%. That used in iron and steel increased by 51.4% and in general manufacturing by 68.8%. The rate of growth of coal used in coal, gas, and electricity production rose at about the same rate as did the production of coal itself. But that used in transportation increased by 385.7% for railways and by 609.1% for ships' bunkers.

In general, then, the failure to increase coal consumption in England was not in any obvious way due to the failure of the coal industry, in spite of growing problems in technology and labor. It seems that coal was doing its job as the major source of energy for all transport, industrial, and domestic use, that it was the single largest employer in the country, and that its exports stood just behind those of iron and steel as the third most valuable to the nation. This is not to say that its performance could not have been improved: It resisted technical improvements and it resisted organizational rationalization, both of which could have made it a vastly more efficient industry. But there is little indication that there would have been an increased local demand for the coal had this been done. It was already relatively cheap energy.

This conclusion accords with the general position taken by Landes (1969:350) concerning the general performance of Britain in the last years of the century. Rejecting the views of Cairncross (1953) and Rostow (1948), he argues that the relative domestic underinvestment was principally because of little demand. The demand for increased investment – as, apparently, with increased coal – came from abroad, not from home. Moreover, in the welter of explanations that have been offered to account for the economic decline of these years, no one, to my knowledge, has suggested that the price of coal inhibited growth.

Table 3.2. *Categories of coal consumption, 1869–1913 (in millions of long tons)*

Categories of coal consumption	1869	1887	1913	% increase, 1869–1913
Generation of energy				
Gas works	6.3	9.5	18.0	185.7
Electrical works	0	?	5.0	
Coal mines	6.7	10.9	18.0	168.7
Transport				
Railways	2.8	6.2	13.6	385.7
Coastal steamers	1.2	1.5	2.6	112.7
Bunkers	3.3		23.4	609.1
Industrial productions				
Iron and steel	14.0	15.3	21.2	51.4
General manufacturing	44.9	58.7	75.8	68.8
Combined	58.9	74.0	97.0	64.7
Domestic households	18.5	28.3	35.0	89.2
Export	13.0	31.7	98.3	656.2
	14.9[a]	35.0[a]	94.3[a]	532.9
	10.3[b]	23.3[b]	73.4[b]	612.6
Total coal production[b,c]	110.7	162.1	310.9	180.8
Total coal consumption in Great Britain	97.7		212.6	120.7

Note: All figures are from Taylor (1968:39), unless otherwise noted.
[a] Calculated from Deane and Cole (1967:216).
[b] Calculated from Mitchell and Deane (1962:121).
[c] Data are from different sources; "totals" will not be the same. Total is given solely for general order of magnitude.

If we examine what constituted the decline (see Table 3.4) in the rate of coal use, we find that it seems to occur almost entirely in the major heavy industries. Beginning about 1870, a decline began in the number of blast furnaces (Deane and Cole 1967:228) and in the value of ore being produced (1967:227). The annual rate of increase in pig iron production for the 20 years before 1875 was about 4%; from 1870 until 1907 it averaged only 2.2%. The total increase in production from 1875 to 1907 was 56% (1967:225). Pig iron exports increased regularly to 42.1% of total exports in 1865–9 and then fluctuated between 40%

Table 3.3. *Comparison of growth of use of steam engines*

	1840	1850	1860	1870	1880	1888	1896
In Great Britain							
Standing steam engines	350	500	700	900	2,000	2,200	2,300
Locomotives	200	700	1,400	2,140	3,200	3,500	5,100
Ship steam engines	70	90	350	1,000	2,400	3,500	6,300
Standing steam engines in:							
Great Britain	350	500	700	900	2,000	2,200	2,300
Continent	100	220	650	1,860	3,270	4,150	5,310
United States	360	600	800	1,220	2,200	3,300	3,940

Source: Mulhall (1899:545).

and 32% until 1900. Some other industries suffered in this era. Coal exports increased consistently except for a brief pause from 1870 to 1875 (1967:216).

Another index of this may be seen in the growth in numbers of different types of steam engines in Great Britain in this era. Table 3.3 shows that the growth of the use of steam power in Britain was in locomotives and ships rather than in standing engines. The comparable increase for the rest of the world clarifies the degree to which Great Britain did not continue to expand its standing engines – those principally used for industry. The United States had a comparable number in 1840, but by 1870, Great Britain had only 75% as many, and by 1896 it had less than 60% of the U.S. number.

Problems of organizational efficiency were evident in the iron and steel industries as well as in the coal industry, as Britain's share of the world's iron output declined from 53.2% to 38.5% between 1871 and 1884. Being displaced by more rapid development of open-hearth processes in the United States, Germany, France, and Belgium, and losing the iron rail market to steel, Britain joined in a market-sharing agreement with Belgium and Germany in 1883. Its proportion of the market was to be 66%, with 7% and 27%, respectively, allocated to the other two. Although Great Britain had experience in such associations, the agreement fell apart a scant three years later (Clapham 1932:151).

If we examine the energy flow significance of these data, the result is clear. Energy used as a trigger to release even greater flows of energy was yielded by the mining of coal itself and by the production of gas and electricity (although some of all of these forms went into direct household consumption). Thus coal production and energy production both increased by about 170%. The portion dedicated to the iron and steel industry and to general manufacturing (both of

Table 3.4. *Estimated distribution of coal in the United Kingdom (as percentages of U.K. coal tonnage raised)*

Users of coal	1840	1869	1887	1913
Iron industry	25.0	30.0	16.5	11.0
Mines	3.0	6.5	6.5	6.5
Steam navigation	1.5	5.0	12.5	6.0
Gas and electricity	1.5	6.0	6.0	8.0
General manufacturing	32.5	26.0	26.0	22.5
Domestic	31.5	17.0	17.5	13.5
Exports	5.0	9.0	15.0	32.5

Source: Deane and Cole (1967:219); detailed citations in original.

which are important as further triggers to energy flow *inside* the country) grew by only a third of the rate of coal itself. The portion facilitating exports and imports (bunker) increased significantly, as did rail use in Britain. But although coal for British industry grew very slowly, coal for foreign industries increased by about 600%, so that by 1913, as much or more was exported than was devoted to British industry. (Figures vary on exports, with Deane and Cole [1967:216] and Taylor [1968:39] favoring a higher figure and Mitchell and Deane [1962:121] a lower one. See Table 3.2.) In short, energy as a trigger for further energy flow at home was diverted abroad, where it surely contributed to greater energy flows elsewhere.

The reasons behind the apparent decline in Britain's position will be found in a wide variety of intricately interrelated factors. Of immediate importance was the more rapid expansion of the United States and Germany. That this was related to their later entrance into the race is generally accepted by various economic historians (cf. Habakkuk 1962, Musson 1965, Saul 1969). Attempts to identify the proximate factors that were operating yield to the difficulties implicit in Hobsbawm's analysis (following the lead of Habakkuk): "The commonest, and probably best, economic explanation of the loss of dynamics in British industry is that it was the result 'ultimately of the early and long-sustained start as an industrial power.' It illustrates the deficiencies of the private-enterprise mechanism in a number of ways" (Hobsbawm 1969:187–8, quoting Habakkuk 1962:220). British entrepreneurs found sufficient profits in the aging industrial establishment at home; they did not need to expand, to re-technify. They "lost sight of the general interest of the economy." "The Great Depression," concludes Hobsbawm, "was, alas, not great enough to frighten British industry into really fundamental change'' (1969:191). The people who were most frightened were not the industrialists but the British landed gentry, and their concern stemmed from the doubts as to their colonial role and the solidity of the class structure at home. But those who had not already long since invested in the industrial establishment were no more likely to do so now than they had been before.

Hobsbawm's general perspective is that it is inherent in the free enterprise system for the pursuit of profits to lead people into those paths that promise the most individual profit and that in the case of Britain these were not apt for the ''interests of the economy'' of the nation as a whole. British industrialists were, in short, to be found lacking when confronting this great national challenge.

Perhaps it is true, if one wishes to take an excessively nationalist position, that the British entrepreneur ought to have acted to promote the growth of the nation. But when seen in the light of diverse alternative systems, the general British response has to be regarded as rational. They generally did what seemed to be best for their own businesses or families; and they certainly, as I shall argue shortly, did what was good for the growth of the world economy. Hobsbawm's own data, however, show that Britain's portion of the world's industrial output consistently declined from the late eighteenth century on. No mere entrepreneurial failures or successes in the late nineteenth century have any serious effect on this trend (cf. Hobsbawm 1969:Diagram 23; see also Berg 1978:612–13 for further support of Hobsbawm).

Although I pursue the matter further in Chapter 9, perhaps it is appropriate here to question why, if British entrepreneurs ignored national needs, they should be particularly faulted. Hobsbawm's assertion that capitalists characteristically seek their own profits would seem to apply to all capitalists; there is no reason to expect British capitalists to differ markedly from others. Rather than moralize on alleged British capitalist failures, the real question is, Where did the responsibility lie to see to the national interests? Certainly one answer is with the national government. Perhaps a more strategic question, then, is to ask, Why did not the government take steps to see to the nation's development?

A search for proximate factors to explain the decline in the use of energy in Great Britain yields a clear picture. There is no doubt that there was enough coal – the principal energy source – being produced during the period until World War I. The evidence shows that the leveling off of coal use was supplemented by a continuing increase in its exportation. In addition, the coal industry paralleled other primary industries in being slow to modernize. However, the most direct factor lies in the fact that not only was the total consumption leveling off, but the portion consumed by industry fell below that used by other sectors, from 53.2% of the total in 1869 to 31.2% in 1913 (Table 3.2).

The importance of coal lay in the fact that it was the indispensable efficient

Table 3.5. *Working power comparison for the end of the nineteenth century*

Country	Millions of foot-tons daily	Manpower (%)	Horsepower (%)	Steampower (%)
United Kingdom	47,810	5	18	77
Belgium	4,470	9	19	71
Germany	38,630	9	27	64
France	30,670	10	31	59
United States	108,200	4	43	53
Russia	45,300	14	66	20

Note: Water power omitted.
Source: Mulhall (1899:464).

cause for societal growth and development. In late-nineteenth-century Britain it was the major resource for expansion. Since coal production did not limit the industrial consumption of coal, the circumstances that were responsible must lie in decisions at home to hold back on industrial expansion and on promoting the exportation of coal abroad. Of all the industrializing countries, Britain depended far more on this source of work than did the others (see Table 3.5).

Pursuing the way energy works can be done most effectively in terms of tracing what happens to the triggers, the controls and regulations. Every energy form has the potential to simultaneously work and carry information. Whether a particular form acts in a work capacity or in a trigger capacity depends on the context as well as the characteristics of the form. Besides the home production of energy forms, Britain had its own human population as an important form of trigger energy, as well as its imports and exports.

4. The world structure expands

A central part of the argument set forth in this essay is that Great Britain invested abroad rather than at home and that this was done as part of an ecological necessity to build an economic and political environment congenial to its own industrial expansion. Since it is an approach not much in evidence in the literature on British history of this era, I want to make one last tangential series of observations as a background to the larger argument. There are many who still do not regard the world structure as an essential component of the history of nations. I can hardly hope to convince them with the limited arguments available in the present case, but I do not think it is out of place here to try to characterize something of the nature of this structure. This chapter is not an attempt to trace the extrainsular history of Britain and its formal and informal empire but rather to examine the general structure of the world that it played such an important part in building.

One must question to what degree the United Kingdom's position as the first industrial power in the world was a matter of real concern to most of the actors at the time. For much of the nineteenth century, Britain's primacy may have been assumed in the minds of many of its natives. This may have been similar to the ethnocentrism and patriotic enthusiasm that leads people of various nations to make similar claims from time to time. Put in another way, how many British citizens were ready to sacrifice their private fortunes and position to keep their country in the primary spot?

In keeping with the assumption that investors invested where they anticipated the best returns, an interest in the welfare of any particular social entity or geographical territory would be based on the presumption that it would help yield better returns. Because the export of British products and the access to necessary raw materials in foreign areas played a central part in the success of many British endeavors, it is entirely logical to expect that British investors would be interested in remodeling other parts of the world to better answer the needs of industrializing at home. In the eighteenth century, there was not one industrialized country in the world. As the first industrializing power, Britain faced an environment that did not initially yield the raw materials easily or respond as a market for the industrial products.

The pursuits of economically active British investors were always aimed in two directions. On the one hand, their efforts were vaulting Britain into the forefront of industrial development; on the other hand, they were determined to create an environment hospitable to this development that would assure returns on their investments. As dependency theorists have never failed to point out, this process often worked against some of the interests of those parts of the world that were the object of industrialist expansion. On the contrary, world building was intended to be beneficial to Great Britain, or, more accurately, to British investors. What is sometimes omitted from discussions of dependency is that industrialization has to begin somehow, and this is one way it may begin. The creation of a new disciplined labor force, of the infrastructure necessary for providing power, transportation, and services, is introduced as a part of this process. Dependency, by its very nature, was an intrinsic component in the creation of an interdependent world structure. Although the British investor of the nineteenth century had to be concerned with building the world structure, Britain obviously did not invent or produce the world structure alone. As other emerging nation-states developed their own industrialization, they contributed increasingly to the same process.

The term "world structure" refers to both a logical category and an empirical phenomenon. The first is derived from the necessary interconnectedness of the human species. The spread of humans over the face of the earth in the preagricultural era created a "world system," a huge, loosely articulated netting of chain mail. This was a structure, but it was one that permitted no centralized action and one in which events in one part would seldom be felt in distant sectors. The empirical phenomenon of the past 400 years, however, has become much more closely knit; many links of the chain mail have been replaced with more direct and far-reaching centralized connections and interdependencies.

It has not been easy to conceive clearly the nature of this immense structure. As if confronted with some vast, all-encircling, Rorschach cast on a planetarium's concave hemisphere, each observer has tended to read into it individual perceptions and problems. It is often denied its own dynamics because, unlike many living structures with which we are familiar, it has no single central nervous system, no fount of final appeal and knowledge. As I argue later, this kind of anarchic organization is too often mistaken for an absence of organization.

The aspect of its nature that has probably been much more difficult to comprehend, however, is that this great assemblage has many of the characteristics of a dynamic dissipative structure. What distinguishes a dissipative structure is that it is constituted by the very inputs that sustain it. We are accustomed to thinking of nations as entities that swallow up the natural resources and inputs available, and that yield living human beings and goods as the product. This vision, however, is based on the model of the manufacturing machine, which consumes and produces but remains relatively inviolate. Social structures, however, are composed of the chemical and mechanical converted forms taken as the inputs, and thus they are usually as vulnerable as the inputs themselves.

Great Britain should not be thought of as a piece of geography that merely witnesses the flow of goods and people; it is itself that flow. The island is an environmental segment that houses and provides some of its resources. The territorial identification, however, makes Great Britain relatively easy to conceive. The world structure cannot be identified territorially but must be seen almost wholly as process, as the flow of goods and people and their chemical conversions into products and other people. To make this clearer, let us spell out some of the major characteristics of this larger world structure.

World structure as composed of individuals and groups

The major members of the world structure are contemporary nation-states, along with the external economic (usually, but not always, capitalist), political, social, military devices that are intended to increase inputs, to control greater portions of the environment, and to articulate the parts. Before the advent of Western colonialism, there simultaneously existed on the earth surface autonomous societies at significantly different degrees of evolutionary complexity – that is, bands, chiefdoms, and early kingdoms and their imperial extensions. Under these circumstances, individuals often played more visible roles. Pretenders could challenge the chief or king or could flee to remote areas where a new society could evolve from the migrant remnants of the old. During the Christian expansion in the sixteenth and seventeenth centuries, individuals were often called on to be the catalyst in a particular surgent effort at expansion. Spain, Portugal, France, and England all commissioned individuals in efforts to gain new territories that would then pertain to the sponsoring crown. Although today's entrepreneurs still build up private empires, they now have to bureaucratize and subordinate them to national regulations and international agreements. It has been argued that multi- or transnational corporations act without regard to national interests, but this is only partially true. They operate first in their own best interests, but these more often than not depend on some specific national interests. Since they operate in various states, their activities must often be ambiguous and, indeed, ambivalent, because they affect the interests of any particular state. Nevertheless, at times they need to seek the protections that only a nation-state can offer, and then they must take pains to see that their orientation appears to conform to that of their potential sponsors.

Thus the component actors of the world structure are not only the nation-state but also various private and semiprivate individuals, groups, and associations whose respective fortunes wax and wane as their successes and energies permit. All, however, work within a culturally shared model of the world as divided into nation-states. The success of the varying interests is determined by the selective processes of the operation of power structures, controls over resources, natural forces, and chance.

Basic coordinate character of world structure

Although nation-states provide the great conceptual map that serves as the defining framework of relations today, this is fairly recent, and it is not eternal. Even within the scope of current history, shifting blocs of nations with satellites emerge and reemerge. Such shifting also occurs within the nations themselves and in their own interrelations. The nation-states are of widely divergent capabilities and powers. They are ranked and reranked in accord with their strengths and weaknesses, and there is often disagreement on the precise order of these rankings. The power of each is determined by the particular position held in the larger coordinate set of relations at that point in time. Thus sixteenth-century Spain and England were more or less equal in abilities; over the subsequent years, however, one declined whereas the other expanded. During most of the nineteenth century, Great Britain was by far the leading expanding industrial nation, but by the end of the century it was in many respects being passed by Germany and the United States. The particular ranking of a given nation – Holland, France, Portugal in the sixteenth century, or Germany, Italy, Belgium in the nineteenth century – did not affect its status as a sovereign state but was reflected in the treatment accorded it at any point in time.

The nature of the kind of system described here has been explored theoretically elsewhere (Adams 1975:52–67, 217–77), but it may be worthwhile to review briefly some of its central characteristics. All social organizations are either more or less centralized – that is, they have some actions that are determined for the whole by some substructure within the whole – or they are not centralized at all. The noncentralized kind I call "coordinate" because each member of such an organization – whether it is an individual among other individuals, an association among other associations, or a nation-state among other nation-states – has roughly equivalent power, and thus interests have to be coordinated in terms of the operations of neighbors. The arrangement of the whole is anarchical, but this does not mean that it is without order or direction. On the contrary, the fact that each member must be concerned with the others in the course of seeking its own best interests means that there is a structure of reciprocal relations that, like the netting of chain mail referred to earlier, leads the whole to manifest a distinctive structure. Perhaps the most obvious coordinate structure with which we are all daily concerned is the operation of the market (or, better said, the markets). No one would deny that the market has a distinctive structure, but all would recognize that there are aspects of that structure that are changing constantly in a somewhat indeterminate course. There are frequent efforts on the part of individual members to centralize controls, there are negotiations and compromises, and decisions are often made with little understanding of how they were reached. Events in one part of the structure may, through chance, be felt violently at some points and be totally unrecognized at others.

The state of affairs that generally characterizes coordinate structures explains in some degree the problems of analysis attendant on them; for instance, very little ''theory'' as such seems to exist about ''regional integration'' and the problem of ''reductionism'' as a theoretical strategy.

With respect to the first, Keohane and Nye assert:

In the strict sense of theory, there is no such thing as ''regional-integration theory.'' Social science cannot satisfactorily explain or predict events in Western Europe or other areas of the world in which regional integration has taken place. No powerful set of assumptions and ''given'' conditions exists with which one can confidently predict patterns of future change. Novel facts continue to appear, unanticipated, or at least not predicted on the basis of existing theoretical models. [1975:377–8]

Certainly one reason that there is such an apparent lack of determinism in the conduct of such a structure is that the parts are fairly independent and self-seeking in their conduct. A coordinate system is specifically not centralized; there is no top level to which problems can be referred for ultimate decision or action, or which can coerce the subordinates. All behavior is likely to be situationally strategic, and decisions made by individual nation actors will be in accord with their immediately perceived situation.

Because of this, Waltz (1975) is concerned that much of the so-called theory of international relations is in fact not theory about international relations but reductionist statements about the nature of states and their behavior. Propositions concerning them would, then, be part of a theory of states. Since theory stands behind predictions, Waltz seems to be saying what Keohane and Nye say but emphasizing that although theory does exist, it is not about the subject at hand. Balance of power, says Waltz, is the only theory that exists on the higher level (1975:65–70).

Coordinate structures elicit theory that seems reductionistic because much of their behavior is derived from lower-level decision making that often cannot, and does not, answer to factors that operate at higher levels. Waltz is unhappy about reductionism, but reductionism is necessary when what one is studying is itself little developed beyond the parts that compose it. This is a methodological constraint. The problem is to develop theory beyond that available from reductionist approaches, and that means a theory about the formation and expansion of larger structures.

I have argued elsewhere that the world structure, under current circumstances, cannot expect to centralize (Adams 1975:274–8). It is useful to describe something of that problem here. A single, full-scale, centralized structure could only emerge at the world level if international decision makers obtained sources of inputs independent of those provided by the nation-states. Since the component members in this instance are the nations, and since the nations control all resources, there is nowhere else for international leaders to turn for independent resources. This, of course, is precisely the weakness of the United Nations, as it is of all the specialized agencies it has spawned. To the degree that a powerful majority of the members favor concerted action, it can act; but cross-cutting interests frequently make even this impossible.

Theory of coordinate systems can be sought best not in the events themselves but in their interrelations. One direction can be seen in that all members share an inevitable, if occasional, surge to expand in their own self-interest. The stimulus for this usually derives from ecological circumscription in the larger sense. That is, it responds to dangers or threats perceived in the action of other societies or in the changing environment. Their behavior is thus logically predictable, but not pragmatically easy to propose.

Since each of the members in the world structure may at any time be in some unique postures of expansion, we would expect that the world structure itself would be in expansion too, both in human population and in other energy forms and flow being used. Since renewed effort to expand is one of the principal responses to failure, threat, or competition, there are always some portions of the whole that are expanding, even when some others find it unnecessary or unwise.

One must be careful not to rationalize. We must remember that the processes are in large part unconscious and anarchic. Where conscious decisions are made, they reflect the view of the individual decision makers at various levels. Only recently have there been stirrings of concern for survival of the world system and its environment as a whole. Such concern comes rarely (other than rhetorically) from leaders of nations, obviously, since they are concerned about their own domains. And international decisions from the political center of the United Nations more often than not merely reflect individual national interests. Feedback, at this point, comes principally through natural selection. It is manifested by droughts in the Sahara, starvation in Bangladesh, oil spills in the English Channel, the disappearance of entire species of fauna, a shortage of coal during an Indiana winter, the rising price of Maine lobsters of declining size, and so on. In the immense complexity of the expanding world structure, it is not odd to find efforts to seek the devil behind it all and to nail the "guilty" parties that are most responsible. This appears in political guise or as economic factors, and still occasionally in charges of perverted desires for individual eminence. Perhaps the most popular culprit in contemporary literature is "capitalism."

Capitalism as culprit

Identification of capitalism as culprit by a large, often intelligent, and energetic portion of the scholarly community demands some attention. Perhaps as good a case as any to begin with is Immanuel Wallerstein's "capitalist world system" (1974a,b).

Wallerstein proposes that a capitalist world system emerged in the "long sixteenth century" and has since come to dominate the world. The system includes socialist and capitalist nations, but it is the capitalist framework that sets the rules for interaction. It has seen its own particular evolution, and Wallerstein proposes that it has its own three-layered political–economic structure, with certain *core* states being the most powerful economically and militarily, certain *peripheral* states providing the raw materials with cheap labor, and certain *semi-peripheral* states acting as a political buffer between the extremes of haves and have-nots (1974b). If Wallerstein's characteristics can be sustained, it is clear that this is not just an assemblage but a particular continuity of parts that warrant being called a structure. There are some problems with this picture, however.

To label this structure a capitalist economic system is misleading. Wallerstein, in the Marxist tradition, assigns priority to economic relations, specifically to capitalistic relations in the modern epoch. Undoubtedly we are concerned with economic relations, but the world system with which we are dealing is more than a capitalist system; it is also an ecological system and, I would argue, an energetic or thermodynamic system as well.

I do not believe that the emergence of the world structure can be seen adequately as a capitalist event. Critics assert that one consequence of capitalist development is a progressive exploitation of human labor and of the environment. This seems to be an indisputable fact. The question that remains, however, is how much of this is peculiarly capitalist, in the sense that there is some alternative way of accomplishing comparable development that would not involve such exploitation. A school of thought emerged recently that argues for a natural process whereby human populations expand and thereby place increasing pressure on their resources. A common solution to this constriction is to intensify their efforts, to increase their production, and thereby to more rapidly deplete their environment (cf. Boserup 1965; Spooner 1972; Wilkinson 1973). The specific versions of the argument vary from one exponent to another, but the core of agreement is that expansion leads to deprivation, which in turn leads to environmental depletion through more intensified efforts. An additional common reaction is to attempt to strengthen the social organization, usually by centralizing (cf. Adams 1975:149).

Much that advocates ascribe to capitalism is in fact characteristic of the human condition and constitutes a phase of what has been a more complicated and larger process. This is the expansion of the human population, gradually accelerating conversion of the environment and human activity into forms that appear appropriate at the time. Industrial capitalism is the particular culprit, because it has raised the intensification of human growth and destruction of the environment to a new high through combining the profit mechanism with the buildup of inhuman machinery and extrahuman energy flows. Hence, the capitalism set forth by Wallerstein and others is extraordinarily important, but it is not a device that slipped in from the wings 400 years ago and took over the controls and direction of the human condition. In fact, it has been a growing combination of elements, a gradual accumulation of devices and mechanisms that grew together increasingly in postfeudal Europe. Money, credit, banking, the market, impersonal transactions, control over labor, and rights to resources were some of the earlier elements; mechanization, controls of metals, engineering skills, expanding use of fossil fuels, the steam engine, organization of enterprises, and bureaucracies are among the more recent accretions. Today's capitalism would not be possible without transnational enterprise, giant petroleum tankers, electronic information processing, international market transactions that become known worldwide within minutes, and so forth. At every point in the history of capitalism, its particular set of constituents has varied, always growing bigger in conformance with Lotka's principle. The search for better investment opportunities, for ways to be more sure that energy will flow, always accompanies it. The shifting of people and goods from one continent to another is done in the same framework.

The view from the capitalist summit well into the twentieth century was that all was well with this expanding giant. By the mid-nineteenth century, however, the human and environmental destruction attendant upon it was already signaled clearly by Marx, and the evolutionary pattern of which it was a part, by Darwin. The growing combination of elements seemed to work well in a world of apparently endless resources, with an ample "residue of matter and available energy." The problem is that they grew together as a whole, creating a new structure, and it is often difficult to distinguish them. Capitalism has emerged as a catalytic device of extraordinary effectiveness in hastening the flow of energy through human society. We are less sure whether it is an *auto*catalytic device that now runs out of control within the world structure. Although its course cannot be controlled by any nation-state, it can be materially slowed by concerned, collective international action. Capitalism is the most highly advanced complex of energy triggers known in human history, but it is the lineal descendent of the intertribal relations that long juggled peace and war as alternative strategies.

The emergence of a world structure as a necessary adjunct of the more intensive exploitation of resources, of the increasing energy and matter flows, may seem to pose an almost closed determinism. Indeed, when we look at the active role of humans in the process, it seems that most philosophies, religions, and politics have been dedicated to making it grow more rapidly through various states of succession. Many human minds have unquestionably been dedicated to furthering the work of increasing energy flow, the work of natural selection, and hastening the time of crises, success, and failure. "Perhaps, the destiny of man is to have a short, but fiery, exciting and extravagant life rather than a long, uneventful and vegetative existence. Let other species – the amoebas, for example – which have no spiritual ambitions inherit an earth still bathed in plenty of sunshine," suggested Georgescu-Roegen (1975:379). There is little evidence in the United Kingdom (or elsewhere) that the alternatives that spawned the policies of free trade and its opposition, protectionism, have given way to a different concept of the environment. There is no evidence that this nation that was the first to enter the industrial revolution is not still among the leaders in the race to be first out.

What our theory of a world structure tells us thus far is not that the world is coming to an end but that the explosive expansion throughout recent centuries must slow down and eventually end. Until we explore more extensively how such actions come about, we do not have a good basis on which to make any predictions. What we can look at, however, is the British deceleration of 1870 to 1914; for that period contained many events that may reflect the process of taking a slowing down into account. The slowing down was not, however, one more imperial decline in the continuing history of the rise and fall of empires nor one more cultural failure to achieve an ongoing adaptation. Britain's place in the history of the world structure was unique. It was the locus of expansion of the core of the industrial revolution, a process that saw the beginning of world expansion based essentially on the harnessing of nonhuman energy. The concern of this work is with the end of that beginning.

5. Triggering flows: trade, investment, and invisibles

The argument thus far is that Great Britain, for whatever reasons, opted to invest abroad rather than at home, and that this led specifically to a deceleration of energy consumption at home. This export of capital, it is proposed, served to help construct the world structure. In this and the next chapter we look briefly at the nature of that investment and see whether the primary research in this area seems to support these positions.

In terms of energy flow, the important processes are those that promote the circulation of energy forms and their conversion. The first question is not whether British production continued unabated or even increased, but whether this production was destined to promote further flows and, if so, whether within Britain or elsewhere. I argue that the shift from the use of British coal within Britain to export coupled with the increase in investment abroad probably succeeded more in increasing that flow than would have been the case had those components been invested within the United Kingdom. To explore this fully would require time for research that is simply not available. The object, therefore, is to show that it is not only possible but that the research to date is consistent with such an interpretation.

The choice to increase flow outside has two results of theoretical interest. First is that it materially contributed to the construction of other parts of the world in such a way that they too became industrialized, in that they were able to participate more actively in industrial interchange and thereby increase their own flow of energetic materials. The second is that to seek such an eventuality would, under Lotka's principle, mean that Britain was acting in a way that would be favored by natural selection. Thus while Britain was promoting the increase of energy flow, the locus of much of this increase was outside Britain, and hence the benefit of selection was presumably to be felt on the outside rather than in Britain itself. In this way, Britain became a trigger that helped develop the world, although at its own national expense. Direct investment in Britain would have yielded a greater internal activity, but much of this would have been for consumption goods. Unlike circulating more capital, this does not act as a trigger for increasing subsequent flows.

There seems to be little question that the era in question was one of extraordinary foreign activity on the part of Great Britain. Saul holds that "the period from 1870 to 1914 is unique in British economic history . . . simply because it saw the peak of the influence of foreign trade in the economy" (1965:5). Compared with later years, Brown says that this era appeared "as a golden age of the world economy as a whole, and of the British economy also, at least in its capacity as the keystone of the structure of world trade and finance . . ." (1965:46). Both writers insist that these perspectives are too simplified, and therefore possibly misleading, but not inaccurate. British reliance on the rest of the world continued to grow so that "by 1913 Britain was dependent on overseas supplies for seven-eighths of her raw material (excluding coal) and for over half of her food" (Saul 1965:9).

The importance of British activity abroad is generally acknowledged and has been the unhappy focus of many recent studies in colonial dependency and economic imperialism. The importance on the Continent and in the New World of British skills and investment in the earlier phases of the industrial revolution are also well known (Bartlett 1969). The British contribution to the building of modern industry and transport in most important regions outside of Europe was greater than that of any other European power and by 1914, British foreign investment comprised 43% of the total foreign investments of Great Britain, France, Germany, Switzerland, Holland, Belgium, and the United States (Saul 1960:66–7). Before the 1870s, the greatest single portion of this investment was also from British sources. The most accepted figure for the size of this investment is that provided by Imlah, who calculates that between 1875 and 1913 the accumulated balance of credit abroad (minus gold imports) increased from just over £1,000 million to over £4,000 million (1958:80).

Simon has analyzed the composition of these investments and points out that the major portion was dedicated to social overhead capital – transportation, public utilities, and other public works (1967:40–2). Thomas (based on material from Herbert Feis) reports that over 40% of the total was invested in railways, and 40% of that, in turn, was in U.S. railways. Only 14% of the total was invested in raw materials, foreign commerce, and industry (Thomas 1967:14). This means that the greatest part of the British investment abroad was not in the extraction of primary products nor in their manufacture into products; rather, it was in the infrastructure, the enabling devices that facilitated the operation of the whole. Next to railways, another 30% of investment was in government.

It must be remembered that the argument here is not that investors necessarily favored investments that might act as triggers; a trigger would not, in itself, recommend a particular investment, because there is little in it to make it a better investment than another. Infrastructure investments, however, tended to be less risky. Since many specific businesses and units of production had to use railways and electricity and had to pay taxes, such investment did not depend on the particular success of one industry or another. Certainly the very large amount in government securities – 35% of the total in 1913 – suggests that the question of risk was serious. On the other hand, 55% of the total, according to Simon, was in private securities (1967:40). (Simon's figure of 35% for investment in governments is based on more recent figures than is the 30% Thomas takes from Feis's work. See Thomas 1967:14.)

The importance of the trigger process is illustrated in Britain's gains from the so-called invisible trade. These included, besides overseas profits and dividends, the earnings on shipping, insurance, brokerage, and interest. During the nineteenth century, Britain had a consistently negative balance of merchandise trade; this, however, was surpassed regularly by a more than compensatory positive balance both of invisible trade and overseas investment earnings. These earnings did not directly benefit either the British consumer or British industry. Rather, they went to the investor – middle and large scale – who was looking for a way to make money but not to develop Britain. The ratio of invisible trade to merchandise trade remained below 1.5 during the second quarter of the nineteenth century. In 1850 it had been somewhat higher, being above 1.5 more often than below. After 1906 it increased markedly, being over 2.0 until the war (Deane and Cole 1967:35, Imlah 1958:70–5). The importance of this invisible trade lies both in the absolute amount of money that was invested outside of the British productive system and in its being steadily made possible by Britain's heavy reliance on imports. It was given special importance by the bankers, who made it appear that the entire system was successful, since the overall year-end pound sterling balance was in Britain's favor. This reinforced a general perspective that Britain not only could but had to depend increasingly on external development rather than look more critically to its own productive establishments. There thus developed in Britain a capitalist class whose income depended more directly on foreign earnings than on the internal development of Britain at home.

It should be mentioned that the role of British banks was always prejudiced in favor of foreign investments and trade. Some writers have attributed this to the fact that the major British bank owners were of foreign origin and therefore had relatively little knowledge or interest in domestic development (Cairncross 1953:91–2). However, the wholly British Bank of England played a very similar role. Mowat notes that banks in general did not give much attention to domestic industrial development, and it was not until confronted with the disastrous depression of the 1930s that "the Bank of England and other banks came together to form the Banker's Industrial Development Company, to give industry the benefit of the banker's advice" (1955:269).

The growing relative importance of British financial operations abroad as opposed to the role of exporter of industrial products is illustrated by a report by a German commentator in Mexico who noted that between 1850 and 1880 the number of British import houses declined from 79 to 3, and the 3 remaining were primarily active in banking. In contrast, German houses rose rapidly to about 80 by 1870 but were in turn largely replaced by French houses by 1890 (Katz 1981:51).

These are, of course, interrelated factors. The capitalist class, which overlapped the aristocracy as it grew, became dependent on a system that was more promising than simply investing in Great Britain; that is, by investing abroad, they were investing where development was occurring and bringing profits, even though this might lead to competition with British development. The success of this invisible trade not only satisfied investors but gave Britain as a whole confidence in the status of its own system, which was *not* premised on increasing the domestic rate of energy consumption. The success of this paper trade must have helped deflect attention from the basic question of energy control and development. Since the larger system was seen as being dependent on the success of invisible trade, special credibility was given to the City, where decisions about the status of the pound sterling took precedence over the substantive welfare of the national institution.

In the matter of merchandise trade, it is difficult to arrive at a clear set of figures that distinguishes goods exported and imported in terms of their destined role, whether for immediate consumption or to serve as further triggers to additional energy flows. Tables 5.2 and 5.3 are crude estimates that throw some light on the matter, but because they are taken from classifications that were not made with my needs originally in mind, they cannot be expected to examine precisely the interests of this work. With respect to imports (Table 5.2), there is a sharp drop between 1860 and 1880 in the category of raw materials and semimanufactured goods, presumably constituting materials that went into further manufacture. This reflects, perhaps most important, Britain's increasing dependence on foreign production of consumer goods, represented in the category of manufactured and miscellaneous goods. In absolute terms, there was an increase in raw cotton, timber, wool, silk, and other major materials. But there was a disproportionately greater increase in imports of meats, butter, and other consumer goods (see Mitchell and Deane 1962:298–301).

In exports, the picture is somewhat reversed. Table 5.3 categorizes the classes of goods listed in Table 5.1 by whether they were most likely to be destined for final consumption or whether they were intermediate to final consumption, and therefore could be regarded as trigger devices. It will be seen that there is a relative general increase in the latter category and a decrease in the former. Great

Table 5.1. *British exports of manufactures by commodity groups*

Commodity group	£ millions				% share of world trade			
	1880	1890	1899	1913	1880	1890	1899	1913
Iron and steel	21.5	24.3	19.5	37.5	60.5	56.1	49.3	35.6
Nonferrous metals	4.3	6.7	4.6	7.7	38.6	42.9	14.8	10.4
Chemicals	8.0	11.6	12.6	24.0	29.4	26.3	22.8	21.9
Nonmetalliferous metals	2.0	3.3	2.4	5.3	20.6	22.5	13.9	16.8
Miscellaneous materials	4.4	5.4	4.3	8.8	17.0	14.3	11.2	10.6
Metal manufactures	14.4	21.8	31.1	62.8	42.2	42.8	30.6	25.6
Ships & railway material	9.8	17.0	16.0	24.3	80.8	74.9	56.5	48.2
Cars and cycles	—	—	0.7	7.6	—	—	24.1	17.1
Drink and tobacco	2.3	3.2	4.2	9.7	9.8	13.0	18.1	30.5
Textiles & clothing	119.8	124.7	109.9	197.7	46.3	47.5	40.9	41.4
Cultural & entertaining goods	2.3	2.8	3.5	8.4	26.8	19.8	14.3	17.1
Other finished goods	3.5	4.7	6.3	11.6	19.0	19.8	20.0	22.3

Source: Saul (1965:13, Table VI).

Britain basically needed the export market in order to obtain the income to keep its industries going and yield profits to them. These exports did not, as observed earlier, yield enough to pay for all the imports that were brought into the country; the invisibles and overseas investments provided this additional amount. What is interesting, however, is that while Britain was increasing importing consumer goods, it was increasing exporting trigger mechanisms.

Having submitted these figures, I would caution that they are based on pound sterling values of exports and imports, and therefore do not necessarily represent their potential energy values, either as substantive flows or as energy costs for actuating triggers. It is, of course, these energy values that are of real relevance to our argument. They are useful because they indicate a consistent direction of change, not because they give absolute amounts. These data merely suggest that it would be of value to ascertain the comparable energy values.

The major areas where Britain was feeling the effects of German and American export competition were iron and steel and manufacture. Table 5.1 shows a relative decline in their portion of the world market in all of the basic trigger manufactured products. The reasons for the decline in British activity in these markets is certainly complex, and again the search for more proximate causes by economists has not brought any broadly accepted explanation. In any event,

Table 5.2. *Proportions of imports into the United Kingdom, 1840–1910* (*based on £ values*)

Year	Food, drink, and tobacco	Manufactured and miscellaneous goods	Raw materials and s emiman- ufactured goods
1840	39.7	3.7	56.7
1860	38.1	5.5	56.7
1880	44.1	17.3	38.6
1900	42.1	25.0	32.9
1910	38.0	23.5	38.5

Source: After Deane and Cole (1967:33).

Table 5.3. *Percentage change in components of exports dedicated to final consumption and intermediate to final consumption*

Year	% in intermediate to consumption	% in final consumption	% in other	Total
1880	31.2	66.5	2.3	100.0
1890	37.6	60.0	2.4	100.0
1899	40.1	57.9	2.0	100.0
1913	39.9	58.0	2.2	100.1

Data from Table 5.1. "Intermediate to consumption" includes iron and steel, nonferrous metals, chemicals, nonmetalliferous metals, metal manufactures, ships, and railway material; "final consumption" includes cars and cycles, drinks and tobacco, textiles and clothing, cultural goods and entertainment, and other finished goods.

while the British share of the world market in these products declined in almost every category, the absolute export value increased (see Table 5.1). Table 5.3 suggests that it is these very products that became more important among British exports. Thus it seems clear that whether Britain stopped exporting in favor of domestic consumption or something else is irrelevant. Britain was merely overtaken by others in the world market.

The dependence of Great Britain on imports has long been recognized as a major characteristic of its industrialization process, and the pursuit of free trade as a policy was crucial to the flow of both imports and exports. Adopted first in the 1840s, these measures gradually led to the elimination of almost all custom duties or other constrictions on imports and exports. It was a policy that worked effectively on a world that was peculiarly vulnerable to its penetration. The colonies and the uncolonized autonomous non-Western areas may have put up some constrictions, but in general, a local externally oriented class wanted certain British goods and had products that were desired in the United Kingdom.

By the end of the century, the situation had changed markedly. Most world areas were under a protectionist policy, either as national powers or by virtue of being within the colonialist control of some Western nation. The industrial competition confronting Britain had created a climate of increasingly deep concern. In answer to this, there had grown within Britain a strong protectionist group under the general banner of "tariff reform." The position of the Liberals was fragmenting, as some began to advocate a militant imperialist stance and as government increasingly intervened in domestic affairs.

If we are willing to conceive of the United Kingdom as a large dissipative structure, then what had occurred was that free trade and tariff reform were competing to designate the nature and kind of energy processes that should be sought in its best interests. Each policy represented a constituency of British citizens whose particular relationship to the existing energy flows made one or the other more preferable. Free traders wanted Britain to act as a catalytic device for the expansion of the world trade structure, whereas protectionists wanted more direct development of the United Kingdom. As Semmel expressed it, "The Free Traders saw Britain as a small production unit within an international economic organism – say, a brain within a huge, sprawling body – the Tariff Reformer looked upon her as the organism entire, needing brain, and muscle, and senses" (1968:146–7).

Tariff reformers were impressed by the fact that British industry was facing increasingly difficult competition and that British products were having less success abroad while foreign imports were increasingly filling up the local market. "Made in Germany" became a war cry as the products of growing industry and organized peasant craftsmen flooded markets with retail goods as well as industrial specialties. The collapse of the British wheat industry in the 1880s stimulated proponents of protection to a wider effort of propaganda, and as other industries gradually became subject to losses due to foreign competition, the concern broadened. This position was coupled with imperialism and a revived mercantilism, for it was the fast-disappearing, as yet unclaimed, potential colonial areas that provided what was left of a marketplace for free trade. As Germany, Belgium, and France expanded their colonial claims, the free trade areas open to British exports were progressively reduced. Developing greater British self-sufficiency, however, was a major concern in this movement, because imperialism had some attraction for free traders in that it opened the way for greater foreign investments (Macdonald 1967:92; the main body of the argument here follows from Semmel 1968:136–8).

Thus the free trade policy was in Britain an essential mechanism for the growth of the world market, the world structure. In this manner Britain, as a centralized structure, necessarily lost some of its autonomy to the greater role it was playing at the world level. Its dominance in the market for capital, insurance, shipping, premiums, interest, dividends, and so forth, meant that the outputs of the structure that constituted the United Kingdom became the inputs that made possible an important part of the expansion of the world structure. The proponents of free trade, however, were not merely the money men. As Semmel (1968:136–8) and Pelling (1968:7) point out, it also included a very large sector of the working class and some major industries. The "organized working class," whose members could remember the stories of the desperate forties, was strongly for free trade, as were workers in those industries that were parts of the larger world trade process. Great Britain had about one-half of the world's merchant marine, and the British shipbuilders obviously benefited from the whole process; they accounted for some one million laborers. The coal industry did not need protection against foreign competition because British coal was regularly in demand and because, as was noted earlier, exports of coal increased during the whole of the period being examined here. This accounted for another million laborers. The Lancashire textile industries, collectively accounting for some 1.5 million workers, depended entirely on export. Even though markets were closing in those developing countries that were developing their own textile industries, free trade promoted the spread of products to the markets of the Near East and Far East. Add to this the shipowners and some 200,000 seamen, together with some 1.25 million laborers in other transportation enterprises.

Of the major old industries, only iron and steel were on the side of the protectionists. They were suffering from the pinch abroad and from the competition of the cheaper steel and products coming from German industry. The industries hardest hit by the competition from abroad were most of the manufacturing concerns: glass, building materials, chemicals, tin electrical supplies. But in sheer numbers of labor, these were not large industries, and many were new. Thus the free trade position not only had a strong existing lobby, but it was a lobby of hallowed tradition, with the largest of the old industries, together with some of the largest labor forces in Britain. This phalanx had been willing to let agriculture suffer; it was quite capable of letting iron and steel suffer too.

Semmel's similes for the free trade and tariff reform positions – seeing the United Kingdom as *a part* of a whole organism or seeing the United Kingdom as a whole organism in itself – are very apt. As a part of the larger world structure, it made perfectly good sense to consume cheaper foreign goods. But as a whole organism it made more sense to reduce the importation of consumption goods and to increase production, and thus energy consumption, at home. Under both policies, however, it presumably made good sense to export triggers. The decline of the market for iron and steel meant a loss in that particular sector, and that had important consequences internally. From the point of view of providing Britain with triggers to release cash and credit into the domestic economy, however, the export of anything was to the good. Beyond this, the export of triggers promised a much higher foreign activity, which would, it was presumed, work to the advantage of reducing costs of imports. This obviously worked in the case of the investments in foreign railways and infrastructure. American grain did pour from the prairies at a price that was advantageous to everyone except British grain farmers.

It has been long argued among economic historians whether the continued foreign investment, if it had been applied at home, would have served to keep British production and export of such products as iron and steel in the forefront of the world (cf. Cairncross 1953:231–5, Kennedy 1974, McCloskey 1971, Rostow 1948, Saul 1965). Deane and Cole summarize the events as follows:

The evidence indicates, in effect, that at any rate from *circa* 1875, the tendency was for the average levels of foreign and domestic investment to move in opposite directions . . . If . . . one of the reasons for the slackening in the pace of British economic growth at the end of the nineteenth century and the beginning of the twentieth was the growth of foreign competition, it is not surprising that home and foreign investment opportunities tended to appear in inverse relation to each other. [1967:268]

Landes is skeptical of these details and argues that there was no significant domestic–foreign correlation anyway, because people invested wherever the promise of yield was good (1969:356–8). The question seems to me to be unanswerable in terms of immediate effects, but it seems equally obvious that in the long run Britain's mid-nineteenth-century hegemony was going to be lost. The last quarter of the century is the period in which it occurred. The major triggers of coal and cash were increasingly turned abroad, where a much more convincing case was being made for their effect. In terms of energy flow, it is not possible to be sure whether their use abroad or at home would have been more effective in enhancing domestic flow. It seems almost inevitable that the chain effects stemming from foreign use would have yielded a far greater total flow. Moreover, the foreign flow provided the triggers necessary for inputs needed by Britain.

If we look at the whole structure of energy flow in Britain, then, it can be argued that the immediate cause for the decline in the rate of per capita use of energy in Great Britain was that the triggers that would have released the flow necessary to keep up the increase in domestic energy consumption were being used abroad. Their channeling abroad led, in turn, to an important series of increases in world structure flows, which in many instances reverted back to Britain. The whole import–export picture reflects this in some part, but among the more specific items of importance is whether Great Britain and its population generally benefited or suffered because of this course of events. The answer is, as might be expected, that they did both differentially. This question is pursued in Chapter 8.

In more general terms, this analysis argues that in the relation of energy flows to the changing structure of society, the flow of trigger mechanisms is at least as important as the flow of substantive energies. It is probably somewhat meaningless, apart from dealing with specific cases, to argue that the one or the other is more important. Without substantive flows, the basic work of sustaining the society cannot be done. Without triggers, the substantive flows cannot be released. What must not be confused, however, is that triggers are, themselves, also flows of energy, and as such they too are subject to problems of structure and regulation. What does seem clear is that the manner in which the two are handled at any time by the decision-making mechanisms of a society always involves a question of strategy; the way that any particular flow – be it regulatory or substantive – affects another may often be a matter of chance. But it is from such chance events that entirely new structures may, from time to time, emerge (cf. Prigogine, Allen, and Herman 1977).

6. Triggering flows: skills

Most studies of the great movement of population during the nineteenth century have emphasized the rates of change, the flow and ebb of numbers. But it is also important to note that the flow of migrants was also a flow of certain skills. For migrants add not only to the general work force of the receiving country but contribute specifically to its distinctive sectors. Entrepreneurs and skilled workers may be more important for the energy flow they serve to release or amplify than are the straight work inputs of common laborers. In the United States, both were important. It is therefore of value to look at the nature of this migrating population.

General occupational change during this era was significant in Great Britain. Table 6.1 shows that for the total occupied population, the percentage classified as "public administration," "professional occupations and their subordinate services," and "commercial occupations" increased consistently from 4.8% in 1851 to 11% in 1911. This is what might be expected according to our general understanding of structural mobility in such expanding industrial situations. In comparing this overall picture with the occupational composition of migrants, there are some problems of definition. Even with the definitional uncertainties, however, Table 6.2 suggests that the pattern of migration among individuals of various occupations was different from the outset. Most notable is that there is no parallel between labor and the professional categories. The latter start with a rather high percentage in the period 1876–80 and then simply fluctuate over the entire era. These fluctuations in no way parallel the general expansion of the professional class suggested in Table 6.1. Moreover, the general level of 9% to 15% for this class is as high or higher over this period than the 11% that is the highest figure it reaches in the population as a whole. Figures for the change in the agricultural component of the total population show a comparable consistent change, a decline from 27.3% in 1851 to 11.1% in 1911. Again, however, the figures for agricultural migrants show little correspondence to changes in the overall population figures. There is a fluctuation from 9% to 18%, with no very obvious secular relation to the events taking place nationally.

Whatever the total figures, different occupational sectors evidently marched

Table 6.1. *Percentage of total occupied male labor force in various classifications*

| Census year | Percentage of male labor force classified as: | |
	"Public administrators," "professional occupations and their subordinate services"	"Agricultural, horticultural, and forestry"
1851	4.8	27.3
1861	5.2	24.5
1871	6.3	19.9
1881	8.0	17.1
1891	8.8	14.2
1901	9.8	11.6
1911	11.0	11.1

Source: Mitchell and Deane (1962:60).

to different drummers. Thomas, in a now classic study (1973), has demonstrated that the migration from the United Kingdom was particularly responsive to periods of boom in the United States and increased substantially when there was an expansion in railways or in building construction. The total migration figures show a great increase in the 1880s and then decline again by the early 1900s (see Table 6.2). All sectors of laboring migrants follow this pattern, suggesting that they did indeed move to the New World in search of more substantive labor. The interesting aspect is that the variation in the merchant professional component among migrants is much less than that among laborers. Whereas the former vary from 52,000 to 61,000, farm laborers vary from 21,000 to 86,000 and back to 24,000, and skilled workers vary from 78,000 to 142,000. Clearly there is a much more consistent push behind the merchant sector than behind the other sectors distinguished in Thomas's analysis. Of particular interest is Thomas's correlation between migration and the times of demand for labor in the United States, suggesting that pull was more important to unskilled labor than to the regulatory class; the latter continued to leave Britain irrespective of the variations in the U.S. pull.

Data from U.S. records on the arriving immigrants in the United States are not couched in the same categories as those from the British records. Table 6.3 shows a combined percentage classified as "professional" and "entrepreneurial group" as being considerably lower than the British listings for "merchants and professionals." The U.S. register, however, showed a much higher percentage

Table 6.2. *Percentage of adult males leaving the United Kingdom, by occupation (nos. in thousands)*

From Thomas (1973:Table 10)	Total	Merchants & professionals		Farmers & graziers		Agricultural laborers		Total agriculture %	Skilled workers		Laborers & Domestic Servants		Miscellaneous & not stated	
		No.	%	No.	%	No.	%		No.	%	No.	%	No.	%
1876–80	378,919	52.1	13.8	22.0	5.7	21.6	5.7	11.4	77.8	20.5	123.6	32.6	15.3	21.6
1881–5	634,904	61.2	9.6	25.6	4.0	34.2	5.4	9.4	104.0	16.4	282.8	44.5	15.8	20.0
1886–90	648,923	60.5	9.3	32.3	5.0	86.5	13.8	18.8	142.7	22.0	196.6	30.3	9.2	20.1
1891–5	501,504	53.9	10.8	17.5	3.5	48.3	9.6	13.1	111.7	22.3	139.1	27.8	12.9	26.1
1896–1900	394,610	57.7	14.6	16.4	4.2	24.3	6.2	10.4	106.2	26.9	87.2	24.7	13.6	26.1

From Thomas (1973:Table 12)	Total	Commercial & professional		Agriculture		Skilled		Laborers		Miscellaneous & not stated	
		No.	%	No.	%	No.	%	No.	%	No.	%
1903–5	139,684	13.9	10.0	19.4	13.9	31.1	22.3	39.9	28.6	35.3	25.3
1905–10	172,328	17.9	10.4	22.5	13.0	39.1	22.7	45.9	20.7	47.0	27.3
1911–13	171,441	25.4	14.8	30.1	17.6	46.3	27.0	38.3	22.3	31.4	18.3

Source: Thomas (1973:Tables 10, 12).

Table 6.3. *Percentage distribution of immigrant occupational categories to the United States from the United Kingdom, 1875–1930*

Year ended June 30	Professional	Entrepreneurial group	Skilled	Farmers & farm laborers	Common laborers	Servants	Total occupied (no.)
1875	1.6	3.7	28.2	7.1	39.8	17.4	43,815
1876	2.4	6.2	32.0	9.6	30.0	15.7	24,841
1877	2.7	7.0	30.8	11.6	31.6	13.6	19,234
1878	1.9	5.8	25.9	11.7	36.3	15.6	18,507
1879	1.7	4.9	28.8	9.2	39.0	13.7	26,009
1880	0.6	2.3	21.7	7.6	50.3	16.3	78,680
1881	0.9	2.8	20.1	6.6	54.2	13.5	77,656
1882	0.8	2.7	22.2	5.9	54.3	12.7	93,296
1883	0.7	2.0	20.5	5.3	49.4	18.9	83,113
1884	0.8	2.0	22.6	5.5	46.5	19.6	69,344
1885	1.0	2.3	21.8	5.4	46.8	20.5	59,766
1886	1.2	2.8	21.8	6.3	46.6	19.2	63,002
1887	1.0	2.6	22.4	5.3	50.0	17.5	90,545
1888	1.5	2.7	27.8	5.7	45.7	14.4	96,410
1889	1.4	2.9	25.4	5.5	43.6	19.6	83,811
1890	1.9	3.8	22.4	6.3	43.2	20.5	69,567
1891	1.9	4.5	22.6	4.7	42.7	21.9	68,488
1892	1.7	3.1	23.7	5.5	38.5	26.2	61,849
1893	1.5	2.8	28.7	6.0	30.3	29.1	54,892
1894	1.5	2.5	28.3	6.6	23.1	35.6	36,414
1895	1.5	2.2	27.2	5.3	21.7	38.9	48,285
1896	1.3	1.9	24.4	5.4	22.8	41.3	36,452
1897	1.3	1.9	20.7	5.5	22.4	43.0	26,672
1898	1.2	1.5	18.3	5.3	24.7	42.1	29,104
1899	1.7	1.6	15.0	4.8	27.7	45.4	36,754
1900	1.3	1.1	14.9	5.5	33.1	41.5	39,262
1901	1.8	1.5	19.2	4.0	28.9	41.1	33,905
1902	2.0	1.6	20.2	4.9	27.3	40.5	36,930
1903	4.0	3.0	25.9	5.0	24.0	33.1	54,815
1904	6.3	5.8	31.3	4.9	17.3	31.5	655,247
1905	4.8	4.9	32.8	5.3	18.3	32.0	92,203
1906	5.7	4.6	36.5	6.4	17.6	25.5	76,482
1907	5.1	3.4	39.9	5.8	20.2	21.3	80,455
1908	5.7	3.9	35.3	6.5	18.6	25.9	70,976
1909	9.4	6.3	46.7	6.5	12.5	14.2	59,422
1910	7.7	5.3	49.6	7.6	12.7	13.0	81,816
1911	8.1	4.6	49.0	7.2	10.6	14.9	85,444
1912	9.0	5.3	43.5	7.7	9.6	17.6	71,562
1913	9.4	5.1	44.5	7.2	9.4	15.4	79,474
1914	10.4	5.2	42.6	7.4	9.1	15.3	72,675

Source: Thomas (1973:Table 80). Original data taken from returns issued by the United States Bureau of Statistics of the Treasury Department and the *Annual Report of the Commissioner General of Immigration.*

of "skilled" than the corresponding category in the British records. It also appears that a considerably lower percentage of people were reported as being in agricultural work among those arriving in the United States than among those leaving the United Kingdom. From Thomas's data, however, there tended to be a generally larger percentage of agricultural laborers going to other countries and continents than to North America (Thomas 1973:Tables 10,12).

Although the U.S. data do not reflect precisely those from British sources, we can sketch some interesting relationships. The proportion of skilled labor more or less parallels that of the professional and entrepreneurial group, suggesting that the United States classified as skilled those who were seen as professionals in Great Britain. Of greater importance, however, is that the proportions of common labor follow a very different curve than do the regulatory components, the professional and entrepreneurial group. The former hit a peak in the early 1880s, then gradually decline until World War I. The latter, however, fluctuate mildly during the later decades of the nineteenth century, then increase sharply in the first years of the twentieth century. The servants category follows a general pattern similar to that of the common laborers, but the peak comes much later, at the end of the century (Table 6.3). Thus both the U.S. and U.K. records confirm that the flow of professional, commercial, and entrepreneurial sectors was more constant and varied differently than that of labor.

Thomas's material is also interesting in that there are so few agriculturalists (either farmers or laborers); for the literature is consistent in describing the great depression as a period when many people were forced off the land and into the emigrant track. Emigration was evidently a step process; the poorest and least able were ill-equipped to migrate abroad, so they simply moved elsewhere in the United Kingdom. The continuing availability of labor in the United Kingdom supports this. Migrants who went overseas were more likely to be in slightly better conditions, probably in terms of skills and economic capabilities.

It should be noted that among the U.K. migrants to the United States (and elsewhere as well) there was a vast disproportion of nationalities. The overwhelming majority of migrants came from England and Ireland. Some came from Scotland, and very few came from Wales. Given that there were so many fewer natives in Ireland than in England, Ireland felt a much more profound loss. Of equal importance, however, is that the majority of Irish were from the unskilled sector, whereas a more significant percentage of persons from the regulatory classes came from England. The percentage of English migrants that were classified as "professionals" or of the "entrepreneurial group" never dropped below 5% of the migrant population and rose to as high as 23% of the total. Among the Irish, the percentages in these two categories never rose above 5% and were usually much lower. By the same token, the numbers of Irish classified as common laborers and servants never dropped below 60% of the total and reached as high as 86%. Among the English migrants, those classified in these two categories never rose above 57% and was usually much lower. The pattern among the Scottish and Welsh tended to fall between these two extremes but was much more similar to the English pattern than to the Irish, except that among the Scots a smaller percentage of the total fell into the common labor–servant class than among the English (Thomas 1973:Tables 81, 82, 83, 84).

Demographers are concerned with whether migrants are answering a push from within their own country or a pull from another. Thomas's material suggests that before the American Civil War, the migration from Great Britain preceded the economic boom in railway construction, but it surely helped provide the labor that contributed to those expansions. After 1870, however, U.S. railway construction booms seem to have preceded the increase in migration and were in turn followed by an acceleration in U.S. coal output and building construction. Thomas suggests that this shift is a "structural change," although just what this means is not clear. What is clear is that this labor was redundant in the United Kingdom, the emigration from Britain was convenient for the need for labor in the United States, and the early nineteenth-century beginnings were independent of the later construction booms that increased the demand for labor there (Thomas 1973:93).

Considering the population as one of the most important potential triggers for facilitating energy flow, it appears that the skills in the U.K. emigrant population were higher than their proportion in the native population. A thesis that Britain was merely sluffing off its least-useful people could surely be sustained if we were to look only at the figures and trends among the laborers and unskilled population. But the very different pattern followed by the professionals and entrepreneurial class suggests that they were not being sluffed off so much as they were seeking better opportunities for their talents. The consistency in their numbers suggests much more strongly a continuing lack of opportunity in Britain than it does a response to a fluctuating market abroad. If this is so, then it becomes meaningful to note that approximately 285,000 men of this class left the United Kingdom between 1876 and 1900.

We have three sets of data to help us estimate the possible impact of this on the operation of the society. There were in the United Kingdom in 1901 approximately 1,136,000 men in comparable categories. This was almost twice the figure of 522,000 for 1871 (Mitchell and Deane 1962:60). On this basis, it would appear that such a class would have been 20% to 25% larger at the turn of the century had these migrants remained in the United Kingdom and pursued their chosen occupations. Table 6.1 shows that in the adult male labor force, there

was an increase in those occupations classified as professional and public administration from 6.3% in 1871 to 9.8% at the turn of the century.

Chapter 10 presents a slightly different analysis on the basis of total population
figures. In the period 1876–1901, the approximate period during which the
285,000 emigrated, the percentage of the total population that would be classified as regulatory in occupation increased from 5.815 to 6.15 (calculated from
Table 9.2). If the emigrants had remained home, the percentage would have
increased to 6.85, a tripling of the annual rate of change of that percentage. A
glance at Figure 10.1 will show that this would have expanded the rate of increase of the regulation curve by a slight amount. It increases the annual rate of
change of the percentage of the total population over the period from 0.013 to
0.044. At the turn of the century, the regulatory rate of increase (Table 10.1)
jumped to 0.14. In summary, the emigrants would have added a significant amount
to the regulatory population, but not as much as was probably needed if the
British, in both public and private sectors, had seriously tried to increase their
regulatory capacity. In another light, the society was not producing enough regulatory personnel, and yet it was exporting perhaps 20% of them.

7. The case of grain agriculture

A problem with the argument that Great Britain needed to engage in overseas investment rather than domestic investment in the basic industries is that the alternatives require us to engage in "as if" history, which is more amusing than convincing. Moreover, to depend on selection explanations implies that we are not optimistic about the possibilities of detailed proximate explanations. One way to provide sustaining arguments is to show that the processes implied by the selection explanation were in fact followed in other instances by the same people. In this way, the argument follows a consistent rationale and thus must be challenged by equally convincing evidence to the contrary.

The argument here is that Great Britain willingly and (at least to some degree) knowingly sacrificed the redevelopment of its basic industries in favor of overseas investments and developments. In the case to which we now turn, this process essentially took place. Moreover, it did so in a way that contributed directly to the decline of the landowning aristocracy, a weak but certainly not moribund sector of the regulatory apparatus of the country.

During the earlier part of the nineteenth century, British agriculture, under the protection of the Corn Laws and government aids, provided the nation with the major part of its food by evolving one of the more efficient agricultural systems in Europe. The land tenure on which it was based economically supported an important part of the British aristocracy. "In 1873, 18,546,000 acres of England and Wales – almost exactly half the total area of the country – were owned by only 4,217 persons, each of whom possessed 1,000 acres or more" (Ashworth 1960:49). These owners leased to "a quarter of a million farmers who in turn employed . . . about a million and a quarter laborers . . . The richest individuals in Britain continued to be large landlords, deep into the nineteenth century" (Hobsbawm 1969:195–6).

This rich development did not result from an irrational love of rural life by the landowners. Beginning with Peel's Act of 1846, and followed up by further legislation in the 1850s, some £12,000 was advanced to landowners to drain land and bring it under cultivation (Clapham 1932:271–2). Thus the state intervened and made it economically worthwhile for landowners to invest further in their land, and it did so at the very outset of an era of laissez-faire philosophy in government. Given the transport of the time and the comparable developments elsewhere, these men effectively had (in 1868) a monopoly of some 80% of the food used in the country as well as 90% of the livestock needs, and the rate of livestock production was increasing (Ashworth 1960:46). For the landowner, the circumstances were benign, and the prices were sufficiently high that the yield for income tax from land rose between 1851–2 and 1878–9 by nearly 28%, from £47 million to £60 million (Clapham 1932:278).

A series of wars – in Crimea and the United States – helped keep potential import prices high (Clapham 1932:280). By the 1870s, however, heavy investment in foreign railways and grain production, particularly in the United States, made available through the free market a flood of cheap foreign grain, severely cutting into British grain production. This was unquestionably a vast advantage for the poor, but it began a "capitalist agrarian reform" that stretched out over the next 80 years. In keeping with nineteenth-century laissez-faire policy, this reform was initiated and carried out by the operation of the free market rather than by government planning. It not only reduced grain agriculture, but it dealt a blow to the sector of the land aristocracy that was dependent on that production. It also made rural life in Britain untenable for millions of people who were forced to take up urban labor or to emigrate.

About 1870, the world flow of grain expanded and prices dropped through the sharp increase in productivity resulting from agricultural technology on the prairies of Canada, the United States, and Argentina, and also from extensive cheap production in Russia. By coincidence, England suffered a series of serious droughts that forced it to turn abroad for additional grain just as cheap foreign grain became increasingly available. Even without the droughts, however, the cheap grain would ultimately have depressed the British grain market and achieved the same results.

The effect of this change in the market has been argued to have been impressive and systematic. In 1850, about 16 million hundredweight (cwt) of wheat was imported into Britain. By 1868 this had doubled, and by 1878 it had tripled (Mitchell and Deane 1962:98). Between 1872 and 1913, the amount of land in grains dropped by one-third; that in pasturage went up 25%. Wheat imports increased markedly over the next 15 years.[1] The price of wheat dropped from an index of 191 in 1870–4 to 50 in 1900–4. Many landowners, including some 400

---

[1] Ashworth (1960:54) reports that wheat imports increased from 58.3 million cwt to 99.3 million cwt between 1875–7 and 1893–5; Mitchell and Deane (1962:98–9) report an increase of about 49 cwt to 68 cwt in the same era, with an additional increase in wheat meal and flour of 6 cwt to 19 cwt; Hobsbawm (1969:198) reports an increase of about 30% from 197.8 million cwt to 280.6 million cwt between 1870–4 and 1885–9. I cannot at this time explain the vast discrepancy in these figures.

peers who owned more than one-third of the total mentioned earlier, found that grain agriculture was no longer profitable (Ashworth 1960:49, 57). Hundreds of thousands of farm laborers and tenants were forced from the land, and investment in agriculture, agricultural technology, and development all but ceased in grains. The effect was by no means as catastrophic, or even as serious, in all farming sectors; some, such as dairy, expanded. Thus did the market produce an agrarian reform. Landowners who had serious problems in maintaining their estates sold them; others retained theirs in the face of accumulating debts, to fall to a great surge of buying from 1914 to 1927, when a quarter of the land was purchased by tenant farmers and speculators (Hobsbawm 1969:201). This process marked the end of land as the principal basis of aristocratic wealth.

Many descriptions of the effect of the agricultural decline of the landowners and aristocracy suggest that it was both sudden and a severe blow to the traditional conservative class. Whether the change was a disaster or an inconvenience depended a great deal on the competence of the landowner.

In the early nineteenth century agricultural rents had long ceased to be the sole source of income for an enterprising landowner, especially if his estate had industrial or mineral potentialities. Landowners dominated many turnpike trusts, and inland waterways proprietaries; their urban ground rents multiplied as town and industries developed; in many cases they engaged in entrepreneurial industrial activities. [J. T. Ward quoted in Macdonald 1967:86]

Data compiled by Putnam (1976) show a gradual decline from about 83% to 70% in the proportion of landholders in the House of Commons between 1740 and the Reform Bill of 1831. The same slope continues until the Reform Bill of 1867, when a very sharp drop begins. From 1867 until 1910, the percentage fell from about 65 to 20. Similarly, although the proportion of hereditary aristocrats in the Cabinet declined from 70% to below 60% during the entire nineteenth century, a very sharp drop began in the 1890s. This decline in the role of the aristocracy was hastened by the decreasing share of agriculture in the national income, a trend that started in the eighteenth century. The specific challenge of grains, then, in the last quarter of the nineteenth century was merely a component of a much larger picture (Putnam 1976:173–6).

This description of the agricultural scene is, I believe, more or less general knowledge. There are aspects of the story, however, that leave open important questions. The notion that these events were sudden and were solely responsible for the influx of foreign grains does not stand up under examination. First, there had been a significant dependence on foreign wheat and flour for a decade before 1870; the value of those imports varied between 20 and 40 million pounds during that time, and then between 40 and 50 million during the 1870s (Mitchell and

Deane 1962:298). In quantity of wheat and wheat flour, there were more pronounced increases in imports in the 1860s than in the 1870s (Mitchell and Deane 1962:98). Second, even though British agriculture was hailed as extremely modern in this era, the modernization consisted of mechanization and technique, not of a shift in basic energy sources. Thus it was an improvement in efficiency, but not a basic change. Of even greater importance was the kind of agriculture that emerged: the so-called high farming.

High farming was an ecological control system that included the careful rotation of soils between wheat and other crops, thereby avoiding fallowing. There was intensive use of manure and other fertilizers, including Peruvian guano and later Chilean nitrates. Among the important rotational crops were turnips and clover, which were used to feed sheep and cattle and were subsequently converted to manure for the soil, allowing the "intricate interweaving of arable crops and livestock into a combined business whose individual parts supported each other" (Orwin and Whetham 1964:10). Turnips and other root crops were a crucial link between the grain and livestock production from an ecological standpoint; this link was particularly costly in energy of human labor. The land had to be spread with rotted manure.

Harrows followed the seed drills and then came hoers, hand hoers to single along the lines and horse hoers to control the weeds between the rows. Finally, the crop must be lifted and topped, and part, if not all, carted to the homestead for the winter feeding of stalled or yarded cattle. The maintenance of this link year by year taxed the resources of men and horses, with the ploughings and cross-ploughing, the harrowings and hoeings, the cartage of muck and the hauling of roots. Yet a well done turnip crop was vital to the continued production on the improved scale for two reasons: the amount of muck made depended on the winter food available, and the cultivations and manure given to the root crop served the rotation as a whole. [Orwin and Whetham 1964:10]

I am not aware whether the high farming system has been subjected to a serious ecological analysis, but it appears that it was a process that required very large amounts of human and animal labor, and that cash inputs derived from the sale of wheat and livestock. It appears, furthermore, that the structure as a whole would have been quite vulnerable to failures of inputs at a number of points. If there were natural failures, such as in the root-crop linkage, then next year's soil would be unprepared and the animals would go without fodder. If there were any market failures, then the reduction of income would directly affect the large human labor force. Apparently it was an irregular combination of both that dealt high farming the death blow. The market refused to pay the high prices necessary to support the human labor, and the droughts prevented the wheat production that would have been necessary even if the market had allowed it to yield the necessary inputs into the system.

Seen from a distant perspective, British high farming appears to have been a short-lived species of eco-social system that specifically required high inputs of human and animal labor. Although it was combined with mechanization, there was little use of fossil energy sources. The principal use of steam was for threshers, and although these could be afforded only on very large farms, they were supplied more broadly by traveling mills. In an industrializing Britain, where the competition was pushing toward the reduction of human labor input and the elimination of animal power, high farming was a thrust in a direction quite contrary to the sense of the times; it was archaic even as it was coming into being. The combination of droughts and foreign wheat did not only cripple the British wheat system, but it destroyed the high farming system. Reducing the price of wheat reduced the ability to support the human labor that was crucial to the meat–wheat linkage.

Two asides are noteworthy at this point. The decline in high farming was not recognized until well into the twentieth century as a severe loss to Great Britain; especially following World War II, home agriculture once again became of central importance and Britain regained much of its independence in food production. In addition, the high human and animal energy costs of high farming, while contrary to the direction of the industrial revolution, may turn out to once again be of interest if and when fossil fueled agriculture must be replaced by more ecologically sound practices.

Can this shift be interpreted as having increased the energy cost in the production of wheat that reached the British consumer? Since the replacement of manpower by animal or fossil fuel power almost always marks the increase in the total energy input and in the unit energy cost of production (cf. Cottrell 1955), we would assume that wheat produced in the United States under similar conditions, or under those with less human labor intensity, would be more costly of energy in production. If to this is added the energy costs of rail transport to east coast ports and ocean shipping to Britain, it seems inevitable that the unit energy cost of production would be significantly higher for imported wheat than for that produced under the high farming system. The difference in the system is that the high farming system was probably highly energy efficient as an ecosystem. The course of human "progress" to date, however, has consistently sought the reverse of this kind of energy efficiency.

Once the Corn Laws were repealed, the only thing to keep foreign produce out of the United Kingdom was price. When, for reasons only partly within the control of Britain, foreign food prices dropped, there were two alternatives. Britain could again institute protectionism, as the continental European countries did, thereby safeguarding national self-sufficiency with high internal prices; or it could continue its popular free trade policy and let food prices fall. One factor that probably affected Britain's decision was that unlike the continental countries, Britain did not need a large army – it had the navy – and therefore did not need to keep up a population of peasants for a conscript army (Jones and Pool 1940:206). The value of maintaining free trade was clear to employers, who could thereby enjoy cheaper labor. Not only did the agricultural disaster yield more cheap labor, but the decline in prices reduced pressure for wage increases. It is interesting that Hobsbawm's review of these events depicts them as a major error:

This sorry record contrasts with the fortunes of other European countries equally hit by the depression of the 1870s and 1880s, but which discovered ways of meeting its challenge other than that of evasion. [1969:200]

He then cites Denmark, with its "lively and modern-minded farming communities," although he does not cite Germany and France and other continental nations whose protectionist policies retained peasants as cannon fodder. He continues:

The truth was that as in so many other fields of British activity, the economic structure of the pioneer, admirably suited for its purpose in the initial stages, had become a fetter on further development. [1969:200]

Compared with the American prairies, the agrarian structure of Britain in 1870 certainly was not pioneering in the same sense that its industrial development was.

On the general level, the greater flow of grain made possible by the imports not only had the advantage of being cheaper, but it released British capital for investment in more profitable ventures outside of agriculture. Thus the free trade product was one of greater flow, which in itself acted as a trigger to release yet further flows. In terms of world energy flow, the squelching of British grain agriculture was, then, a minor energetic sacrifice for a much greater yield. As compared with the earlier action of Peel to promote farming, the government action reflected a change in policy. But the change only recognized that the growing trade of Britain was broadly more productive of energy flow than was British grain agriculture.

In fact, the decision to let agriculture suffer the consequences of the changing world was a positive decision by the Conservative Disraeli administration. It was not allowed to slip by. The investigative commission that examined the situation produced "an inconclusive document . . . chiefly interesting from the difficulty which the commissioners evidently felt, and which was shared by their contemporaries, in distinguishing between long-term trends in the industry, such as stretched back into the 1860s, and incidental events such as the outstandingly poor harvest of 1879" (Court 1965a:38).

It seems likely that the Disraeli decision reflected the immense political difficulty in Britain to move to protectionism. Of course, in this particular instance, it was hard on the peers who were dependent on agriculture, but even many Conservatives were not dependent on agriculture, and those peers that looked to the future were moving into business and industry.

It is important to remember that agriculture produces what people eat. When goods are not scarce, economists, like other people, tend to take them for granted. (Air was a favorite illustration of a free good, until we began to understand smog.) In the years before 1870, Britain had been favored with both abundant provision of food and prices that pleased the landlords. Cheap foreign imports were a threat to the agricultural industry, not to food supply. Because the dependence of the United Kingdom on foreign imports was long-standing, the question of national self-sufficiency probably did not loom as large as what might, in today's terms, be seen as the advantages of a very cheap energy source. The shift was from agriculture as a preindustrial industry to food as a world business. Imports of food were advantageous to the very important "invisibles," both in terms of shipping and in the extensive and increasing British investments abroad. The decision to avoid protectionism was in keeping with a vision of Britain not as "that of a great landlord proprietor" but "that of a great merchant" (Ashworth 1960:1, quoting an 1868 statement by Dudley Baxter).

Looking at the energetic structures involved, we have a case in which the greater structure – the world structure of production, trade, and markets – took precedence in the British decision over a much lesser set of structures – British agricultural production. It reflects the selective advantages in Lotka's principle of increasing energy flow, but the specific impetus was the presence of more advantageous investments favoring the larger over the smaller. Decisions about energy flow are made by the particular sectors that control those particular flows. Britain's control of the seas made the external flow secure; the dominance of commerce at home made the input desirable; the basic industrial needs at home made them advantageous.

Looking at energy flows, it is clear that the shift to foreign grains placed in operation a system with a much greater series of links, a much more extensive use of energy in the world at large. Thus in long-range terms, this can be argued to have been the most logical choice from the point of view of natural selection. Why that choice was made, however, is reflected in the fact that it served a much wider immediate range of British interests than would a policy of protection. The release of energies in foreign areas channeled not only grain for consumption to Britain but yielded returns in cash profits for investors and cash advantages to the general population by affording it cheaper bread.

In terms of the general principle set forth earlier, the course of agriculture reflects the result of channeling energies so as to condition the environment, to create an environment adequate to the input needs. The British choice now becomes clearer; since it chose to condition the world as a structure rather than to expand internally, the immediate payoff came with the dividends from investment in foreign agriculture and the avalanche of cheap grain. Internally the British grain sector could not compete, and Britain thereby became increasingly dependent on the external inputs.

The purpose of retracing the course of grain agriculture in this era is to suggest that the British were not loath to destroy an entire industry, even one of major interest to members of the "ruling class," if that industry seemed to stand in the way of better investments and profits. Thus assertions that individual investors should have had the interests of the nation at heart rather than their own short-term concerns is fairly futile moralizing. There is no reason to think that the welfare of the iron and steel industries would have wrung any more tears from these investors than did the welfare of high farming and grain agriculture.

8. Advantages at home

The regulatory devices that release or inhibit flows of energy within and between societies are complex and of many forms. In the next chapter we look at the most easily recognized regulatory apparatus: the government. In preceding chapters, I argued that the regulation implicit in the operation of the world market, given the advantages in Britain's controlling the seas, being free of destructive wars, and having many home resources on which to draw for energy and labor, allowed Britain to have full advantages of free market operations. In this chapter we look at the reaction of the people, the degree to which the people living in the United Kingdom enjoyed a system that was running sufficiently well that labor could be expected to go on laboring and that people could be expected to go on producing, socializing, and preparing their children for the tasks of surviving in that particular society.

Thus far our attention has focused on the advantages that accrued to the investors. It is also important that population growth not only provided ample labor but posed serious survival problems for many; and their only real solution was migration. The general level of living of the lower classes of the population was extremely low: Studies in the latter part of the century by Charles Booth (1889–91) and Seebohm Rowntree (1902) revealed that at least a quarter of the population was clearly below a subsistence level of income. The extent of misery was broadly ignored by the upper sectors until these and other studies and movements began to bring public attention to them.

Severe unemployment was a periodic fact of life in the fluctuating booms and busts of the late nineteenth century, and in Great Britain it was always potentially present because of the policy of keeping a positive balance of payments. The Bank of England systematically increased interest rates whenever it detected an expressive outflow of gold from the country, even though such payments might result in serious depression of industrial or commercial activity. The inevitable result of reducing economic activity was to increase unemployment (Lewis 1978:35, Thomas 1973:182). Why, under the circumstances, did not the British body politic seek drastic action? Why were they not moved to revolt or revolution? Revolution proved to be an admirable regulator in eighteenth-century France.

Table 8.1. *Improvement in real wages and basketful that average wage earnings would buy, 1860–95 (in percent)*

Country	Annual rate of improvement in real wages	Increase in size of basketful average wage earnings would buy
United States	0.95	78
Germany	1.09	84
United Kingdom	1.92	91

Source: Brown and Browne (1968:160–1).

A full answer to this is much more complicated than can be handled here. It involves why different countries act differently and why the pattern of such actions changes over time. We can, however, look at one particular feature of the British case: whether these movements of investment abroad, of calculated unemployment at home, and of declining position in the world market also made things better or worse for most of the population. The answer is that in the matter of living standard, they were an apparent boon.

Much attention has been paid to the standard of living of past centuries. It seems that not only was Britain's situation not disadvantageous, but during the last part of the nineteenth century it enjoyed the most rapid rise in level of living of any of its major competitors. Cole and Postgate (1963) argue that "between 1873 and 1896, when prices touched bottom, average money-wages over all trades rose a little – perhaps by 5 percent. This meant, in view of retail prices, a rise in real wage-rates of 35 to 40 percent. At the least the purchasing power of the average skilled worker in full employment increased by one-third" (1963:441–2). In a major comparative study of levels of pay and standards of living, Brown and Browne concur that there was an important rise in real wages (Table 8.1). Moreover, they assert that "the rise in real wages through the fifty years before the First World War was most significant of all in its lifting of households over the poverty line" (1968:162).

Since estimates such as these are subject to problems, I have examined the course of change in real wages among the United Kingdom, the United States, and Germany during this era. Table 8.2 gives relative indices taken from different studies of the three countries, all adjusted to an index of 100 for 1914. It shows that the increase in real wages in the United Kingdom was much more rapid than in either of the other two countries, reaching and exceeding an index

Table 8.2. *Comparison of real wages in Germany, United States, and United Kingdom, 1871–1913*

Year	Germany			United States				United Kingdom		
	(1)	(2)	(3)	(4)	(5)	(6)	(7)	(8)	(9)	(10)
1860				64	62	61		55	47	
1870				58	67	63		60	59	
1871	51	66	73							
1875	67	83	83							
1880	61	71	71	68	74	74		69	69	69
1885	68	85	82							81
1890	74	87	87	94	94	94	94			93
1895	80	92	89				95			100
1900	85	99	98				92			103
1905	88	95	96				97			97
1910	92	97	98				99			98
1913	100	100	100				100			97
1914							100			100

Notes: Index of 1914 = 100 (1) Desai (1968:36), Desai's estimates of real wages. (2) Ibid., Kucznski's estimates of real wages. (3) Ibid., Phelps Brown and Hopkins's estimate of real wages. (4) Long (1960:Table 21), Long's figures for real annual earnings. (5) Ibid., Aldrich's data for real daily wages. (6) Ibid., Weeks – Bulletin 18 data for real daily wages. (7) Douglas (1966:Table 146). (8) Bowley (1937:Table VIII), estimate No. 7 of wage–cost of living. (9) Ibid., estimate No. 6. (10) Ibid., Table VII, estimate No. 6.

of 100 by the turn of the century, whereas both other countries did not reach 100 until 1913. Real wages started out much higher in the United States, principally because free land was available and the production from land generally provided a good living. Thus labor was scarce, and wages higher (Habakkuk 1962:11). Even with this advantage, however, the situation in the United Kingdom led to a faster increase in real wages than abroad. While our figures do not allow an exact comparison, the real wages in Germany seem to have been somewhat better in the 1875–80 period, but again, the increase in Britain was more rapid.

The superior British showing in wages would be readily understandable if British production had been at a higher level than that of its competitors. Table 8.3 suggests, however, that this was not the case. As would be expected, the British industrial production index advanced more slowly than did that of Germany and more slowly than did the index of manufacturing of the United States. This, of course, is what we would have anticipated, since the two foreign nations passed Britain in a number of industrial areas in the latter part of the period.

Table 8.3. *Comparison of indices of industrial production and*
manufacturing in Germany, United Kingdom, and United States,
1860–1913

Year	Germany	United Kingdom	United States
1860	13	31.7	9
1870	19	40.2	16 (1870–4)
1875	27	46.7	18 (1875–9)
1880	26	50.3	27 (1880–4)
1885	31	52.1	33 (1885–9)
1890	40	63.3	41 (1890–4)
1895	49	66.5	48 (1895–9)
1900	61	80.1	68 (1900–4)
1905	70	85.7	86 (1905–9)
1910	86	85.5	101 (1910–13)
1913	100	100	

Sources: Germany and U.K.: Mitchell (1976:355–6), indices of industrial production; U.S.: Clark (1957:Table VII, facing p. 335), index of manufacturing.

Finally, studies of food and diet in this era also show that the increase was not
only in purchasing power but that the mix of purchases diversified and generally
improved from a nutritional standpoint. Bowley's estimate for the budgets of
median families in 1860 and 1914 are given in Table 8.4. There is a shift in
both quantity and quality of diet. First there is an absolute increase in the caloric
intake in everything except bread, potatoes, and suet. The quality follows the
general pattern asserted by Bennett (1954), a diversification in foods and less
reliance on starchy staples. What is particularly important is the shift toward
foods of higher-quality protein. If sugar, bread, and potatoes are classified as
inferior-quality foods from this standpoint and the rest as superior, then the shift
in diet can be seen in comparing the caloric intakes derived from the two classes
of food. The caloric yield from inferior-quality foods stays essentially the same
– about 68,000 calories consumed for both 1860 and 1914 – whereas the caloric
yield from higher-quality protein increases from about 20,000 to 38,000, reflecting dietary improvement.

The series of decisions that led Great Britain to invest in the wider world in the
nineteenth century rather than to reinvest at home did not, at the very least, result
in a decline in the standard of living in Great Britain. Quite the contrary, the
figures suggest that it led to the most rapid rise in the standard of living of the
three major competitive countries in the international market. An important rea-

Table 8.4. *Estimated budgets for median families in 1860 and 1913*

Food	Unit	Calo-ries per unit	1860: Wage = 20s 6d.				1913: Wage = 35s 6d.			
			No. of units	Price s	d	Calo-ries con-sumed	No. of units	Price s	d	Calo-ries con-sumed
Bread	4 lb.	5,000	10.5	5	3	52,500	10.5			52,500
Potatoes	1 lb.	310	35	1	7.5	10,850	21			6,510
Suet	1 lb.	3,540	1.5		9	5,310	1		7	3,540
Rice	1 lb.	1,630	1		10.5	1,630	3			4,890
Bacon	1 lb.	2,685	1		10.5	2,685	1.5	1	5.5	4,028
Meat	1 lb.	1,200	3	1	7.5	3,600	10	7	1	12,000
Butter	1 lb.	3,605	0.75		7.5	2,704	1.5	1	9.75	5,408
Margarine	1 lb.	3,525	0	0	0	0	0.5		3	1,763
Cheese	1 lb.	2,055	0.25		2	514	0.75		6.75	1,541
Milk (fresh)	1 pt.	406	8		10	3,248	12	1	9	4,872
Tea	1 oz.	0	2		6	0	8		10.75	—
Sugar	1 lb.	1,860	2.5	1	0.5	4,650	5		11.25	9,300
Total for food				13	9	87,690		22	7	106,350
Sum of bread, po-tatoes, and sugar						68,000				68,610
Sum of high qual-ity calories						19,690				37,740
% of calories of high quality						22.5				35.5
Caloric value per "man" per day						3,240				3,926
Rent				3	0			5	0	
Fuel				1	0			1	6	
Clothing				1	6			2	6	
Sundries				1	3			3	11	
Total				20	6			35	6	

Notes: Family = man, wife, and three children, or 3.87 "men." Blank spaces indicate no data. s = shilling, d = pence.
Source: After Bowley (1937:Table IX).

son why there was no revolution at home – no matter what other factors may have been at work – was that conditions were clearly improving. There was great support for free trade because it was working to the benefit of the average British individual, in spite of the unemployment, in spite of widespread poverty that existed in many areas, in spite of the virtual destruction of the British grain agriculture and the destitution of many rural laborers, and in spite of the failure of the iron and steel industries to grow at their earlier rates. Irrespective of the justifications one may have of German policies for Germany or U.S. policies for the United States, the policies followed by Great Britain seem justified for Great Britain in terms of their yield to the people of the country.

This is not to argue that the increase in living standard can be traced singly or directly to the course of investment. We know that wages did not improve remarkably in Great Britain and that the greater part of the improvement in living standard was due to the constant decline in prices until the close of the nineteenth century. Indeed, the fluctuation in the first years of the twentieth century was due to an increase in prices. Price decline, however, also occurred in the United States, where the cost of living fell from an index of 170–80 in 1865 to 98–124 in 1890 (Long 1960:60). In Germany, too, the cost of living index declined, although irregularly, from 106 in 1871 (with a rise to 113 in 1875) to 99 in 1885, with a rise to 100 in 1895 (Desai 1968:36). Indeed, all of central and northern Europe experienced a general price decline during these years, with an increase early in the twentieth century (Mitchell 1975:736). The conclusion, presumably, must be that the factors that determine the quality of the standard of living are only indirectly tied to the relative expansion or decline of the use of energy. They also answer to other factors that lie more profoundly within the culture and the economy, the minds and the aspirations, of the people.

9. The regulatory weakness of government

I have intimated that I am not in accord with the position taken by some historians that it was the special fault of the British investor and entrepreneur that British industry failed to keep up its world position in the latter part of the century (nor is McCloskey 1973, but for different reasons). Irrespective of what more obvious considerations may have guided them, the direction chosen was not strongly opposed by the majority of the British population nor by the government. This does not relieve us of the question of possible responsibility, however, unless one accepts a monolithic determinism that shapes events quite apart from human interests and decisions. On the contrary, it is precisely because events operated in the direction of these interests that Great Britain did as it did. It may be asked, however, whether in the long run this was the most advisable direction and whether, even given the knowledge of the time, there were not some crucial or key regulators who might not have been able to divert some events to the advantage of internal development. The Bank of England played a central part in keeping the balance of payments always in Britain's favor, and this was through careful calculation and intent and done through decisions made by individual human beings.

Today, if we were to ask what party has greater ultimate responsibility than any other for the welfare of the whole nation, the answer would be easy and immediate: the government. Why did the government seem to do nothing about this gradual decline in Britain's place in the world? Why did it let so many skilled and capable people leave the country? Why did it let so much investment move abroad rather than dedicate it to the redevelopment of home industries? Why did it not institute better technical education? I have already suggested why it let grain agriculture go down the drain and, with that, have obviously suggested part of the answer to some of the other questions. But the fact that a large part of the population may be for or against something can never be the only guiding concern of a government; it also has to look at what may be good for the country over the longer term and to find ways to exercise this leadership, often in spite of popular disapproval.

The argument of this chapter is that Britain did not face conditions that made it clear that there was such a problem until the last quarter of the nineteenth century. When the problem of relative decline did become apparent, there was a growing opposition to free trade politics and to government inaction. Moreover, the government did exercise controls in areas of its major interests – for example, in the maintenance of a positive balance of payments. In most other affairs, however, increasing regulation developed in Britain outside of the government rather than inside it. But perhaps most important was that major interests with contrary notions could not make themselves heard in government until the popular voice became more widely heard through broadening the franchise and building a governmental infrastructure of funds and personnel to handle the activities implied by greater intervention.

If the United States and Germany succeeded in industrializing and becoming international competitors, and if Britain's general trade and financial balance of payments remained good in spite of the expanding role of the competitors, why was Britain undergoing such social contortions about its "declining" position? This must be seen in terms of the social structure and the changes it was undergoing as a part of the growth of the world structure.

In relations with the United States and Germany, the early nineteenth century was a period of exporting British skills and technology as well as British capital and products. For much of the period before 1870, the United States was Britain's best customer and chief supplier (cotton being the major import to Britain). It was also the major destination of U.K. migration. What must be recognized about these two foreign countries is that until 1870, they were themselves suffering severe defects in their own unity. The growing industrial economy of the U.S. North was clearly differentiated from the South, and the issues that led to the Civil War were tearing increasingly at the efforts to knit a national state and achieve a national policy. Germany was composed of a series of minor kingdoms. As long as Britain could deal with the unassembled German states and the United States in terms of a semidisarticulated American South, there was little issue in retaining a superior position in the world at large.

These advantages ended in the 1860s. The Civil War brought a national unity of action to the United States. A part of that was to establish the first major U.S. protective tariff, which brought an end to the particular British–U.S. relationship. Bismarck in the same era launched a unified German imperial state in direct competition with all of its neighbors. Some, such as France, Denmark, and Austria, were defeated militarily; others, such as Britain and the United States, it sought to beat in their markets at home and abroad.

The progress of consolidation in Germany and the United States took rather different paths. The United States had an open frontier, a broad area whose conquest was inhibited only by technologically inferior Indian populations, a weak and technologically inferior Mexico, and a weakly populated Canada. The United States was its own best market and resource base. Quite the contrary to feeling threatened by Great Britain, foreign investment was welcomed and foreign products were bought as needed. Germany, on the other hand, was territorially constricted within Europe and felt clearly the constraints of circumscription (cf. Carneiro 1970).

While circumscription is not the only reason that people may choose to centralize their controls and decision making, it is probably by far the most important. As long as there is no cause for concern about the survival of the society or its government, and as long as the environment presents no threats that cannot be handled with the kind of regulatory apparatus in existence, there will be little reason to centralize. But if it is perceived that obstacles are arising that require a more concentrated strategic focus than is possible under existing mechanisms, then efforts will be made to reorganize society in order to bring decisions more effectively to bear on the matter.

A major difference between the social-structural emergence of Germany and those of Britain and the United States was precisely this issue of circumscription. Germany's response was to create a highly centralized state in which the major plans for development were early sponsored and therefore controlled by the growing central government. This led to the special sponsorship of such industrial efforts as the Krupp manufacturing interests and the protection of peasant agriculture by tariffs. Germany's entry into the business of world colonization was similarly centrally directed, and its search for external resources and markets was much more the venture of a single national state than of a variety of independent enterprises.

In contrast, the U.S. and U.K. expansions occurred without the same sense of circumscription, so free enterprise played a much more important role. Private enterprise in the United States was even more independent in its expansion than it was in Britain, but in both nations the government's role was mainly to facilitate private interests rather than to sponsor or control them directly for the immediate interests of the nation-state. This was possible for Britain because until the 1860s, the world was an open field for its economic imperialism. It was possible for the United States because its own West was wide open; but with the end of the Civil War, California began to mark the limits of U.S. territorial expansion.

Thus what happened in the 1860s was not merely that the United States and Germany began to press closely on Britain in industrial and foreign market exploitation. It was that these two nations found a new degree of national consolidation, a new degree of internal articulation that enabled them to compete on a centralized national basis. This was "political" in the sense that it was the consolidation of the regulatory devices in these countries that began to deal with their own societies as national societies. The United States saw defeat of the Confederacy following the defeat of Mexico; the establishment of protectionism; the winning of the West, which brought vast areas under federal control; and the beginning of land grant colleges. Germany saw its own unification under Bismarck, the increasing exports of its products, the establishment of national school and university systems to promote its own internal development, and the construction of the major military machine on the Continent.

Contrary to the experiences of the United States and Germany, Great Britain during the middle years of the century pursued the laissez-faire principle with considerable enthusiasm. The 1860s and 1870s, however, brought into sharper vision the events in these other nations and the costs that were increasingly being attached to the process of intensive primary industrialization at home. Awareness of events abroad came through the series of military victories of Germany on the Continent, following fast on the military ineptness shown by the British and French forces in the Crimean War; by the growing awareness of foreign competition in the international commercial markets; and by the displacement in the home market of British products by those produced abroad – especially in Germany. The course of financial events also began to yield failures, particularly in the 1870s and 1880s, that drew increasing attention to the complex economic processes that were under way.

The awareness of increasing costs at home came from the growing deterioration of Britain's physical environment and condition of the human population, the recognition that high levels of poverty and misery subsisted throughout much of the most successful and wealthiest country in the world. Increasing problems of public health, food control, destitution and poverty, and urban filth were generally pushed back to the local authorities. Even more visible at the national level were the growth of Irish nationalist activity, the advent of women suffragettes, and the growth of strikes and labor organizations (Dangerfield 1966).

In the political arena, there were two answers to the combined events from inside and outside of the country. These were what Semmel (1968) has linked together as socialist imperialism, the pressure to take a much more militant stand in controlling the world structure and to introduce social measures at home. The second of these necessarily implied a much greater role for government than had been conceivable under laissez-faire philosophies.

It would be misleading to argue simply that British laissez-faire was a cause of slow government action. The evidence is that the government did begin – as early as the 1830s – to take an increasing number of steps, first in public health and laboring conditions, then in education and public utilities, and its action to promote agriculture has already been cited (cf. MacDonagh 1961, Parris 1969).

But the British experience was an early one. National governments were emerging everywhere, but nowhere had one of them confronted conditions like those Britain faced, and to cope with them required invention. In fact, what happened in Great Britain was that the amount of regulation of activities did expand, at a rate not unlike that of other growing nation-states. The specifically British course, however, was that this increased regulation did not lead to the rapid centralization of regulation. The nation-state government did not take on the regulative responsibilities but instead encouraged the growth of local government and private social efforts to answer the needs wherever possible. This, of course, was not the only alternative. Germany instituted far more central government intervention, especially in matters concerning workers' insurance and benefits. The United States also intervened little and encouraged private efforts by entrepreneurs, but it opposed more strongly the formation of secondary structures, such as labor organizations, and promoted public education much more strongly.

Until the mid-nineteenth century, the tax base of the central government was "customs and excise duties on a few items of food and drink, with stamp duties and income taxes the chief of the direct taxes which provided about one-third of the total tax revenue" (Ashworth 1960:23). Local governments depended principally on immovable property. This meant that the central government depended on indirect taxes that had to be paid by consumers – all consumers, thus placing the poor in the position of providing a considerable part of the support. "In the first half of the nineteenth century the outstanding financial task continuously performed by the government has been to redistribute a small proportion of the national income from the poor to the rich" (Ashworth 1960:218).

Between 1870 and 1914, public expenditure in the United Kingdom increased from about £67 million to £192 million. This slightly more than doubled the expenditure per capita from 2.24 to 4.92. Table 9.1 shows the approximate allocation of these expenditures. Of particular interest is that the percentage allocated to the civil government almost doubled in this period.

The increased government income stemmed from the gradual growth of income tax and death duties, with a concomitant decrease in customs duties as the policy of free trade had its inevitable effects. There were, of course, other government revenues, such as those from the post office, but most of these were expended in services. By 1914, the combination of income taxes and death duties equaled the amount received in customs and excise taxes. There was, therefore, a gradual increase in progressive taxation, although a significant amount continued to be borne by the general public; and this situation did not change.

Civil government costs fluctuated between 16% and 20% until just after the turn of the century, when they jumped significantly to almost 30% in 1911. (The percentages given for the "main constituents of civil government" in Table 9.1

Table 9.1. *Distribution of public expenditure for United Kingdom, 1870–1914 (nos. in millions)*

Year	Total gross expended (£)	Total population	Armed forces costs		Total expended in civil service (£)	% of total in civil government	% of main constituents of civil government				
			Total expended (£)	% of total in armed forces			Works and building	Salaries, etc., of public depart- ment	Laws, justice	Education, arts, & sciences	Colonial consul & foreign
1870	67.1	31.26	21.5	32.0	11.0	16.4	8.5	14.9	38.6	14.7	5.0
1880	81.5	34.62	25.2	30.9	16.9	20.7	8.3	13.0	38.5	23.7	3.6
1890	90.6	37.49	32.4	35.8	17.6	18.8	8.8	12.3	30.4	33.9	4.1
1900	143.7	41.16	69.6	48.4	23.9	16.6	8.3	8.7	17.6	51.1	7.1
1910	156.9	44.92	63.0	40.2	41.4	26.4	7.4	7.2	11.1	43.2	4.6
1914	192.3	46.05	71.1	40.1	56.8	29.5	5.8	7.6	8.8	34.3	2.6

Source: Mitchell and Deane (1962:397–8).

merely suggest the general direction of the spending in these areas, relative to the total. Of special interest is that even though education was handled by local governments, the subsidies from the central government were all important and represented an increasing portion of the civil budget.)

Peacock and Wiseman, in a brief survey of the era, hold that the ''Old Liberal'' view ''dominated through most of the [nineteenth] century: all government expenditures were to be kept at a minimum consistent with the provision of adequate protection against the Crown's enemies and of the maintenance of law and order'' (1961:35). Parliament was concerned primarily with raising revenues, not with seeking to spend them. The proportion of the gross national product dedicated to public expenditures remained at about 11% from 1841 until 1900, when it jumped to 15%. Peacock and Wiseman point out an interesting aspect of the quality of these expenditures that perhaps better reflects the relation of government to the society than the citing of quantities:

A remarkably large part of the total government expenditure during the period represented transfers to private individuals (such as national debt, poor relief) and to private institutions (such as grants to private schools). National debt interest payments were much the more important of these. Direct share of government in the national product, therefore, was considerably smaller than government expenditures as expressed as a percentage of national income. [1961:39]

In other words, apart from the military and debt payments, the major expenditures were for the poor, in a system that was kept to a minimum and required almost no centralized bureaucracy, because it was entirely carried out locally.

Turning now to the growth of government employment, the problems may be divided into a number of segments. First is the question of regulation in the society as a whole, regardless of location. The evidence is that personnel in regulation in the broad sense did expand more rapidly than did the society as a whole but that the major increase is evident after 1901. Second is the question of centralization of activity in government, presumably marked by a disproportionate growth in government. The evidence here is that the government did not seriously centralize until after the turn of the century.

If regulation in the country as a whole is seen to include not only the governmental processes but also those of business, industry, and the entire market mechanism as well as the development of professional services that act to direct decisions of individuals, then there is a pronounced increase in the portion of the total population engaged in regulatory activity, as Table 9.2 shows. It should be noted that the universe here is the total population of Britain, not only the economically active portion.

Table 9.3 analyzes the population in the regulatory sector in terms of their

Table 9.2. *Population of Great Britain in human energy sectors, 1841–1971*

Human energy sector	1841	1851	1861	1871	1881	1891	1901	1911	1921	1931	1951	1961	1966	1971
Total population (in 000)	19,194	20,939	23,138	26,025	29,710	33,028	37,093	40,831	42,769	44,795	48,854	51,284	52,304	53,803
Human energy sectors (relative %)														
Transformation	26.96	29.73	32.68	30.23	27.03	25.94	26.05	24.92	24.12	23.85	21.96	20.17	19.31	17.55
Regulation	3.12	4.06	4.04	5.68	5.95	5.98	6.15	7.51	8.74	10.01	13.47	14.13	15.39	15.73
Transport and storage	1.11	1.91	2.14	2.30	2.52	3.41	3.86	4.06	4.89	5.09	4.70	4.46	4.51	4.14
Maintenance and reproduction	68.26	62.91	58.83	60.99	65.46	63.97	63.46	63.34	62.45	60.44	59.82	59.97	60.37	61.42
Other	.55	0	1.13	0.86	0	0	0	0	0.49	0.65	0.36	0.71	0.33	1.18
Total	100.00	98.61	98.82	100.06	100.96	99.30	99.52	99.83	100.69	100.04	100.31	99.44	99.91	100.02
Human energy sectors (absolute numbers)														
Transformation	5,176	6,224	7,561	7,867	8,032	8,568	9,640	10,175	10,318	10,682	10,728	10,345	10,098	9,444
Regulation	599	851	935	1,478	1,768	1,974	2,275	3,070	3,738	4,485	6,581	7,445	8,050	8,465
Transport and storage	212	399	497	601	749	1,127	1,428	1,659	2,092	2,279	2,296	2,351	2,361	2,225
Maintenance and reproduction	13,103	13,173	13,611	15,872	19,448	211,294	23,541	25,865	26,709	27,074	29,223	30,760	31,576	33,044
Other	105	308	262	224	0	0	0	0	210	291	174	376	170	626

Note: Calculated from the census of the population.

Table 9.3. *Analysis of regulatory sector in percentage portions dedicated to public administration, commercial operations, and professional services, 1851–1921*

Year	Total (000)	Public administration Including armed forces	Civil government alone	Commercial operations	Professional services	Regulatory Sector total
1851	486	26.7	13.8	18.7	54.5	99.9
1861	631	30.7	12.0	20.9	48.3	99.9
1871	810	29.3	14.0	26.8	44.0	100.1
1881	1,052	22.1	11.2	34.5	43.4	100.0
1891	1,323	22.4	12.3	35.9	41.6	99.9
1901	1,743	22.7	12.6	38.6	38.7	100.0
1911	2,234	24.3	14.4	40.1	35.6	100.0
1921	3,047	23.0	15.2	48.9	28.1	100.0

Source: Mitchell and Deane (1962:60–1).

general regulatory functions, insofar as the occupational categories of the census permit. This shows that the portion concerned with commercial operations increases consistently, whereas that concerned with professional services declines. Thus until the turn of the century, the significant growth in regulators was in the private sector. The figure for public administration, including the armed forces, fluctuates between 22% and 31%, and the major element in the variation lies with the armed forces. The portion involved in civil government fluctuated slightly, between 11% and 15%. There is, however, a clear tendency toward an increase after 1901.

These data support the notion that there were important changes in the larger regulatory sector of the society, but that these were primarily in the growth of private business and industrial operators until the turn of the century. Government, as a sector, did not begin to grow significantly relative to the entire regulatory sector until that time. Abramovitz and Eliasberg (1957) argue that the figures for the latter part of the century do not accurately represent the growth of government, and instead of an increase of from 2.4% to 2.8% for the period 1851–91, the increase is from 2.4% to between 3.4% and 3.8%. (There is an absolute discrepancy between the armed forces figures of Abramovitz and Eliasberg and those of Mitchell and Deane [1962]. One possibility is that Mitchell and Deane excluded overseas troops. If so, it means that a very large proportion of the army was on overseas duty – 64% in 1851 and 41% in 1891.) If the armed forces are excluded from these figures, the increase is even more marked: It more than doubles from 0.7% to 1.7%–2.1% (Table 9.4). Since Abramovitz and Eliasberg correct only the 1891–1911 and not the 1851 figures and only suggest that so big a correction would not have been necessary at the earlier date, we cannot be sure just how much real change they are suggesting. In any event, the increase in annual rate of increase between the two periods, 1851–91 and 1891–1911, is still very high in the Abramovitz and Eliasberg estimates, from 0.035% to 0.15%, or over four times as high in the later period.

These authors make an important observation (supported by both the census and their own figures): Growth in government personnel in the nineteenth century was larger in local than in national government. This accords with our general understanding of the development of public administration of the time. Education and poor relief, especially, were areas that were handled mainly by local authorities, although under central government controls. While these authors' figures argue for a more important increase in the second half of the nineteenth century than is indicated directly by the census figures, they agree with the much larger increase in government personnel after 1900 that is indicated in Table 9.3. Thus both figures for public expenditure (Table 9.1) and for personnel in government (Table 9.3, Figures 10.1 and 10.2) are in accord that the major upswing in central governmental action occurred after 1900.

It also appears that with the increased income for the government, there was an increase in real benefits allocated to the population. Old age pensions, health insurance, and limited unemployment insurance were gradually instituted, and between 1897 and 1912–13, "the cost of social services to the Exchequer rose by some 25 million, or 1¼ percent of the national income" (Hutchinson 1950:68). Including local taxation, it was estimated that this would yield an increase of 6% in the collective income of the recipients.

The benefits that were coming into being were made necessary by development, by expansion. Besides the urban and industrial crowding and related public health issues, industrialization made illiterate labor a national liability; elementary education became a basic necessity for a government that wanted to have communication facilities to exercise power over its people. Closely related to this was the problem of protecting labor. Victorians were increasingly subjected to the results of studies on the ills of industrial society (Booth 1889–91; Rowntree 1902); these gradually led government commissions to study the problems and to report and make recommendations to Parliament. Ultimately, Parliament would act. With this, a small bureaucracy was created. The nature of the

Table 9.4. *Changes in public administration as percentage of labor force, 1851–1911 (nos. in thousands)*

Public administration sector	Census figures				Census figures corrected by Abramovitz and Eliasberg					
	1851		1891		1891		1901		1911	
	No.	%	No.	%	No.	%	No.	%	No.	%
Armed forces	178.8	70.4	249	40.6	249	44.1	423	44.2	343	26.9
Civil central government	40.0	17.0	906	22.0	105–15	20.4	155–65	16.7	271	21.3
Local government	31.0	12.2	72	17.5	150–200	35.6	350–400	39.1	660	51.8
Total government	253.9		411		504–64		928–88		1,274	
Total labor force	10,447		14,682		14,682		16,605		18,509	
Percentage of government workers in labor force		2.4		2.8		3.4–3.8		5.8		6.9

Source: Abramovitz and Eliasberg (1957:19, 25).

conditions turned out to be worse than anticipated, which in turn led to more professionalism and more action. This process (see MacDonagh 1958) constitutes one kind of interplay and feedback that may occur as a government increasingly confronts problems in its own expanding society.

Abramovitz and Eliasberg have further suggested that there were many important steps taken in the nineteenth century that were necessary preliminaries for the emergence of a more active central government. Centralized government action requires information on which to base decisions. The many commissions of inquiry during the century increasingly cast light on the conditions of the society. More important, economic and social sciences were hardly developed to provide more systematic information. Of greater importance is that it was the business class that was exercising the major open influence on the government (see Table 9.3). Until wider franchise came in with the Reform Bill of 1867, many of the interests of the householder received little expression. The spread of popular participation in the government was important not only for reasons of ideology but because it was essential to enable the government to be aware of and respond more openly to other than landholding and business interests. The great shift came quickly after the turn of the century, with the enactment of a range of liberal and labor legislation. The growth of the influence of public opinion was an important component of this.

Parris points out that the decline in patronage in the central government was in part a response to the need to make such appointments defensible before Parliament (1969:76) and that in the appointment of ministers, the ability of the individual to speak convincingly before Parliament also became increasingly desirable (1969:120).

The British pattern is evolutionarily interesting because it was always somewhat experimental. It seldom attempted giant strides or set up huge programs. This was congruent with two very important characteristics of the population. One was that they were generally fearful of great government intervention; the other was that the gradual increments made it possible to get used to the government little by little, and thus proceed on that uniquely British road to socialism.

Taylor has examined six specific cases in an attempt to find some logic in the government's choice of particular areas in which to intervene. Laissez-faire dominated policy in trade and railway expansion; direct intervention took place in education and public health; considerably less action was taken with respect to factory laws and poor laws. Taylor concluded that in economic affairs, laissez-faire was the policy, but in other areas it was ignored (Taylor 1972). The argument is not entirely convincing, particularly in the case of railways, which were subject to an extraordinary amount of regulation.

If we look at government action from the standpoint of a general principle – that the individual, the domestic unit, or local firm had the responsibility to do what was in its own best interest – then government intervention is left to the following categories: (1) areas that were of no interest to private enterprise and hence were not likely to be done well (e.g., public health, education for the poor, unemployment payments, old age pensions), (2) cases in which the interests of one segment seemed incompatible with those of another, and some solution had to be found (e.g., factory laws, child labor), or (3) situations in which the unconsidered pursuit of private interests by the individual or firm simply created public havoc (e.g., different gauges of railways, train schedules, railway fares). In short, where no one else was likely to pay the social costs, it was eventually up to the government to intervene (Parris 1969:276). The role of the central government in the development of urban services is illustrative of the whole approach. It passed much enabling legislation that did not require action from local governments, but permitted it. From this there appeared local tramways, electricity departments, local telephone exchanges, docks, markets, abattoirs, concert halls, museums, libraries, parks, public baths, and housing (Hutchinson 1950, 55). In general, the British policy as manifested wanted to keep triggers working, to keep the system in high flow. But in trying to assure the continuation of one kind of flow, it was inevitable that some other flows would be adversely affected. Obviously, compulsory child education and cheap child labor are incompatible; high-cost working conditions and cheaper products rarely go together.

One cannot avoid returning to the fact that Britain was the first to confront many of these problems. Clearly, other industrializing states could look at Britain, as they did, and decide that some of the more hideous by-products of such success were undesirable, indicating state action to avoid them. Britain itself did not usually have this advantage until long after it had made its own decisions. How many of the acts for which Britain has gained a reputation for laissez-faire may in fact also reflect an ignorance spawned by primacy?

Given this primacy, it is not surprising that MacDonagh (1958) depicts a model that essentially consisted of trial and error in British administration-building. Centralization in government, however, was ultimately the only solution to the problem, and, as Hinsley (1962) argues, it was basic to all European countries. In May of 1895 the *Economist* observed that "little by little, and year by year, the fabric of state expenditure and state responsibility is built up like a coral island, cell on cell" (Hutchinson 1950:54).

The process, however, as suggested by MacDonagh's model, was always in response to some obvious failure in the system as it was. In the 1890s, with prices going up and the clouds of depression lifting, the Boer War brought a series of blows that effectively stopped any tendency to relax the centralizing process. Ashworth describes it as follows:

> The experience of diplomatic isolation, temporary but humiliating military reverse, an alarmingly heavy rejection of would-be recruits because they were physically unfit, and some sorry scandals in the conduct of the war encouraged the belief that stronger government was needed and helped to set off a new round of enquiries into practical social improvements which it might achieve. [1960:222]

Ashworth goes on to point out that the principal device that was instituted, especially early in the twentieth century, was an increasing delegation of powers to the executive. The fact that Parliament was becoming more active did not mean that it was becoming more efficient. The debate over measures was obviously a different function than executing them. Legislation increasingly gave wide administrative and regulatory latitude to the executive. It is significant that major interventionist legislation occurred under both Liberal and Conservative governments. As the century wore on, the accusation made by Hilaire Belloc and Cecil Chesterton (1911:8–9 and passim) that the government was really run by a "Governing Group" and that the two parties were basically similar in economic or political policy seems effectively to have been the case. Indeed, this continued to be the case until World War II (discussed in Semmel 1968:232–4). There was much crossing over on many issues, and the need of the weakening Liberal party to find allies among Irish nationalists, coupled with the mutual interests in imperialism manifested in different ways by both parties, allowed those against these policies, such as the emerging labor groups, to stand out by contrast.

As was mentioned earlier, there was an increasing number of areas of government intervention, but as an illustration of the general pattern let us look briefly at some steps taken in education. Education, it will be remembered, is an area that Taylor judged to be purely social, and therefore not subject to the laissez-faire philosophy. In fact, the reasons were surely much more complicated. One issue lay in the fact that much of education was in church control; thus, it was argued, it was being done badly. But of much greater importance was the problem of cultural programming. If a labor force is to be cooperative, it needs in some ways to be educated. Johnson argues fairly persuasively that the great public concern with the depravity of the poor is "best understood as a concern about authority, about power, about assertion . . . of control":

> The concern was expressed in an enormously ambitious attempt to determine, through the capture of educational means, the patterns of thought, sentiment, and behaviour of the working class. Supervised by its trusty teacher, surrounded by its playground wall, the school was to raise a new race of working people – respectful, cheerful, hard-working, loyal, pacific, and religious. [1970:119]

Johnson's assertion receives some interesting support in the contrasting actions taken toward the poor, about whom there was concern for governance because of that illiteracy, and in the education of the middle class. The Education Act of 1870 established in principle that schools should be available for every child; in 1880, primary education was made compulsory. From 1880 on, expenditures on public education increased: 5.1% of the local government budgets in 1875 to 10.4% in 1900 and 17.7% in 1914 (Mitchell and Deane 1962:416–18). From 1870 to 1900, the civil government budget entitled "Education, Arts and Sciences" grew faster than any other (see Table 9.1).

The middle class was being trained very selectively in the so-called public schools, about which the Clarendon Commission in 1861–4 waxed enthusiastic. Observes Murray: "The Clarendon Commission seemed almost oblivious of the changing times for they oozed sentimentality about the advantages to the soul of man from the study of Greek and Latin" (1962:179). Here, apparently, there was satisfaction in programming minds that would perpetuate the culture of Victorian England, not in training them to confront approaching demands of science, engineering, and technology, or in speaking of accounting. The purpose of school at both lower and middle levels appears to have been to inculcate conformity to higher principles. In essence, the middle class could be trusted to promote an educational system in this vein for themselves; but for the lower classes, it was up to the state. This suggests that the separation between the state and labor was excessive; and it is not odd that the latter should have evolved such profound distrust for the former. On the other hand, the state policy was obviously preferential for the middle class, and no problem was likely to arise there.

The imperfections in this picture were not uncriticized at the time. Matthew Arnold, inspector of schools, wrote scathingly of the

spectacle of a middle class cut in two and in a way unexampled anywhere else, of a professional class brought up on the first plane, with fine and governing qualities, but without the idea of science; while that immense business class, which is becoming so important a power in all countries, on which the future so depends . . . is in England brought up on the second plane, cut off from the aristocracy and the professions, and without governing qualities. [Quoted in Fores 1971]

MacDonagh recently analyzed the role of British efforts – or lack of efforts – in the development of technology and science, and their relation to actions of the government. He asserts that the government's failure to take a more dynamic and leading role can be traced at least to the 1850s:

The reorganization of universities and schools, of curricula and examinations, at that point, was designed to produce – only more effectively than ever before – the universal man, so trained in the familiar intellectual gymnasium that any later task would find him competent and serene . . . This was a fateful choice, for no opportunity for reappraisal upon a comparable scale recurred before 1914. [1975:516]

It is interesting that the adherence to the public school philosophy has been characterized by critics as an example of the pursuit of laissez-faire philosophy and the establishment of compulsory primary education as an exception to it. In fact, the two seem entirely consonant with each other and with a general policy that kept decision making outside of government as long as things went smoothly. When the state thought that things were becoming too chaotic or dangerous, then it was likely to intervene.

The kind of development that took place in primary education in Great Britain, and the relative underdevelopment of popular secondary and higher education, are one with the pattern of weak centralization that the government itself manifested. I argued earlier that government intervention in national affairs was not simply a matter of the increasing regulatory apparatus in the country at large. Table 9.1 suggests that the growth of regulatory personnel exceeded the rate of population growth. Comparative material affirms that essentially the same pattern of growth of such a broad regulatory sector took place throughout the industrializing world (Adams in press). The issue, then, is that insofar as funding and personnel suggest, the regulatory devices within the British government did not really expand until the turn of the century or after.

This suggests that the reason the British government did not take more drastic steps to institute correctives to the flow of investment funds abroad and the relative decline of their own iron and steel industries lies in the fact that the regulatory apparatus of the government was not sufficiently developed to undertake such action. If pursued, the next question would be why it did not develop such a regulatory apparatus, and the answer would be threefold: (1) The growing sectors of regulation were private and their influence was, if anything, to keep such growth from taking place in the government. (2) There existed no previous model or pattern to dictate that it would necessarily or automatically be the responsibility of the government to face the mounting and novel problems that were confronted by the first industrial society in the world. (3) During periods of crisis – such as the droughts and financial panics – the society as a whole was not confronting chaos or disintegration. Where there was awareness of a relative decline, as in the case of iron and steel, the process was slow and not catastrophic. Until after the turn of the century, with the sudden convergence of a number of growing national problems, there was no real reason for the government to mount a radical change in its mode of dealing with social events.

Put in another way, the government was capable of undertaking the tasks that confronted it insofar as it could deal with them by a process of trial and error, thereby learning what had to be tackled and what did not. This was a slow process, and as long as events did not pile up on one another, it worked. Between the end of the South African War and World War I, however, events did begin to accumulate faster than the administrative capacity of the government could handle them. The problems were not only inside the United Kingdom, but they also concerned the growing international competition and the widespread consequences of industrialism and expanding capitalism. They were no longer solvable by negotiated or legislated action. World War I changed things profoundly. Some issues disappeared; others were postponed, only to arise again in an often more difficult form. In any event, the centralization that had begun in earnest around the turn of the century received a great impetus with the wartime necessities for more effective and concerted action. Centralization came more naturally to the government after the conflict.

The weakness of the nineteenth-century British government may be easier to comprehend if the emergence of the nation-states is regarded as part of the same process as the emergence of the world structure. The flows that simultaneously built the world structure and British wealth also provided the substance for the gradual strengthening of the British government. The difference (see Adams 1975:206–17) was that the growth of the state was a centralizing growth, whereas that of the world structure was as a set of coordinate components. The lack of circumscription of Britain throughout most of the nineteenth century reflected the fact that world structure was not yet far enough constructed to pose a serious threat to Britain's own expansion. The appearance of Germany and the United States as competitors signaled that this era had ended and that Britain would now have to centralize or be unable to cope.

10. The relation of human energy to nonhuman energy

Thus far we have explored the circumstances that contributed to the relative decline in energy consumption before World War I and have concluded that contrary to having a pernicious effect on the population at large, there was an impressive improvement in quality of living. Does this mean that the leveling off in the society's ability to do work had no significant influence in the social structure? If this were the case, then much of the reason behind the present exercise would be lost. The purpose of this chapter is to suggest that the change in energy consumption did have a very important and fundamental effect on the nature of British society, but that the exploration of this opens another field of enquiry, the further pursuit of which must be left for another time. The form of analysis developed here must be followed up in a comparative context before we will be able to evaluate its implications. What follows brings the substantive portion of the present study to a close but, I hope, indicates some directions for future research.

The analysis of human energy sectors

It must be remembered that our general purpose here is to understand better the relation between energy process and the structure of complex society. The first question we must explore is the use of energy in society.

What is energy used for? There are surely as many answers to this question as there are motivations for framing it, but our concern is how energy is used to perpetuate the society and/or the species. The analysis employed here is designed to reveal what one kind of energy use does to affect another kind of energy use. That is, how does the change in the absolute and relative amounts of nonhuman energy affect the use of human energy? We must distinguish between human beings as dissipative structures that need a constant input of specific kinds of energy and society as a dissipative structure that needs not only those material and energy flows specific to human beings but additional kinds of energy that are necessary to the social process.

Energy performs in the social process as it does in all processes; it converts

101

from one form to another. The specific question that frames this analysis is what relation the expenditure of human energy has to these transformations of energy. One such relation is in using human behavior to assure that human energy will continue to be able to be used. This involves caring for oneself and others and preparing to operate as individuals in the society, as well as activities that are specifically directed to the maintenance of the human body and psyche so they can continue to perform. This kind of human energy expenditure we will label maintenance and reproduction, or MR. Although MR affects human organisms directly, human society does not operate merely as an assemblage of organisms. Rather, it utilizes many elements of the environment as extrasomatic tools and implements. These elements are given special shapes and are assigned particular meanings. A great deal of human energy is expended on the extraction of materials and the elaboration of artifacts that extend the action of human arms, legs, and vocal sounds, as well as on the elaboration of goods that are consumed directly. The energy used in the extraction and elaboration of these environmental resources is lost in their transformation, or TR. The fact that all energy use constitutes a transformation should not be a cause for confusion. The sector of activity that we are labeling TR comprises those energy transformations that are used to elaborate products that are then available for human use or consumption.

All dissipative structures are hierarchical and contain various devices and processes that act specifically to direct and regulate the activities of the larger structure and its parts. There is, therefore, in all such structures a certain amount of energy that is dedicated to the regulation of the other energy processes as well as to the regulation processes themselves. This includes decision making and the attendant activities necessary to the carrying out of the decisions. These activities I call regulation, or REG.

There are in addition to MR, TR, and REG other udes to which energy is put; one, transport and storage (TS), is detailed later. For the present analysis, however, we will not explore any further uses. It should also be clear that both human and nonhuman energy can be used in the course of the activities that comprise each of the categories. Of interest to us here is the analysis of human activity. Unfortunately, data from Britain are limited at the moment to the total nonhuman energy, which is not differentiated into these categories over the historical period being examined (e.g., Table 3.2). Table 9.2 presents the results of the analysis of human energy, but before turning to it, we should look more specifically at the categories being used in the analysis.

Transformation

Some part of human activity must always be devoted to the extraction and conversion of elements of the environment into forms available for human consumption. What economists have called primary and secondary sectors both engage in this process. Production and consumption, however, are basically economic concepts, not energetic concepts. That is, production is a change in energy forms that is marked by an increase in value, whereas consumption is a change that is marked by a decrease in value. Thus production and consumption have no real place in an analysis of energy only. Rather, they are both ways of looking at a cultural aspect of transforming energy from one state into another. Both primary and secondary economic sectors are involved in the transformation of energy from a state of less utility to one of greater utility, but both, because of constrictions set forth in the first and second laws of thermodynamics, also involve energy consumption in the sense that some portion is used up and converted to a nonusable form. Hence, in the present analysis, the term "transformation" is used in preference to the economic terms. Similarly, the economic distinction between primary and secondary sectors has a societal significance because it differentiates the early industrializing effect of reducing rural labor while industrial labor was increasing. In energy terms, however, the differentiation is arbitrary, and the two are included together.

Regulation

The regulative activities in human society are very complex and occur at all levels, and there is no way that I can see to capture all of them in any single index or measure. There are, however, entire sectors of complex societies that are dedicated to such activities, and they may be differentiated. Thus we single out those activities that have to do with public administration, armed forces, and police, both at national and local levels; in addition we include people concerned with the economic transactions that channel goods from one part of society to another. All commercial and business operations that have to do with the marketing of goods are thus included in the REG sector. The market itself is a major regulatory device. It is usually not manipulated by the direct action of a single decision maker but is the product of a collectivity of decision makers. The regulatory sector of the society does not, therefore, comprise only the elite but the entire body of white-collar workers that are part of the making and carrying out of decision processes, both in public administration and in commerce.

Transport and storage

This is a clear empirical category, but its practical separation from the rest is made difficult because of its ambiguous nature. It is clearly a process whereby goods and people are transferred from one part of the society to another, and it could, therefore, be included in the REG sector, as is the white-collar group.

But it also involves the physical transfer and maintenance of goods, and therefore it plays a direct role in the TR process, albeit in a negative sense. Finally, since it is the device whereby things are brought to ultimate consumption, it could conceivably be included in the MR sector. As a result, it is easier to handle this as a residual, transitional category that belongs everywhere and nowhere. As will be seen in Figure 10.1, its course parallels both the REG and TR sectors but it is not as marked in its changes.

Maintenance and reproduction

This sector includes all the familial roles, both on the part of those who are caring for others (e.g., mothers) and of those who are preparing themselves (e.g., infants, children, students). It includes the range of professions that are concerned with activities in health care and (somewhat arbitrarily) the arts dedicated to entertainment. It also includes the range of occupations that are involved in feeding and housing people.

The greater part of MR is comprised of the residual census category referred to in terms such as "not economically active." The detailed classifications are concerned only with occupations that play a role in the market economy or in government, activities for which one is paid. Since, for instance, mothers and kin are not paid, they are relegated to a residue. The problem attendant on this census practice is not that people get misclassified but that the data do not permit a more refined way of examining what these people do. The reproduction and care of human beings is clearly a major concern in the survival of society; but it has been reduced in the definitions of Western culture census takers to being of residual importance. Because of this, the data tell us little about this category.

Human energy sector changes in Great Britain

Received knowledge tells us that in the course of human evolution, the gradual increase in the species' ability to capture nonhuman energy and to convert it into useful products led to a lessening of the amount of human energy needed to guarantee survival. Table 9.2 and Figures 10.1 and 10.2 show the relative and absolute allocations of human energy expended in terms of the three major categories being used here. Figure 10.1 superimposes the relative figures on the curve that described the changing use of nonhuman energy per capita. It is apparent from Table 9.2 and Figure 10.1 that there is no consistent direction in the change in the amount of human energy dedicated to MR, whereas both the TR and the REG sectors show very consistent changes. Specifically, beginning in 1880, the TR sector tends to decline less rapidly, increasing its decline again

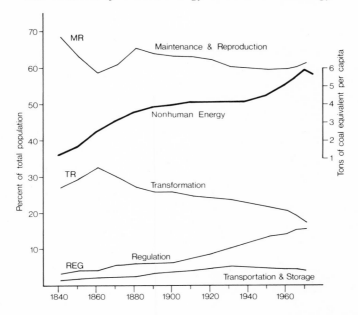

Figure 10.1. Human energy sectors for 1841–1971 and nonhuman energy per capita for 1840–1975, Great Britain. (*Sources:* Nonhuman energy from Humphrey and Stanislaw 1979; human energy sectors from occupational tables of decennial censuses.)

after 1960. This presents a mirror image to the change in the nonhuman energy per capita curve from 1860 on. The REG rises slowly until 1900, when it begins a sharper increase. While there is probably an indirect effect of the energy change being reflected in the REG sector, it is by no means as direct as that suggested for the TR sector.

   To clarify what happened, we must ask more than whether energy was added to the structure. What role did this new energy play in the operation of the structure? The human society changed its form with this increase of nonhuman energy. If we divide the consequence of, or use of, the new energy into the TR/REG/MR categories, we may look first at the performance of the TR curve. From 1841 to 1861 it increases in a manner that is portrayed in Figure 10.1 as being parallel to the nonhuman energy per capita curve. The increase reflects what may be regarded as the phase of the industrial revolution when the increase in nonhuman energy was expanding the production processes such that increasing numbers of human beings were being drawn into the industrial labor process. Sometime around 1870, however, the per capita TR curve takes a sharp downswing and thereafter generally declines.

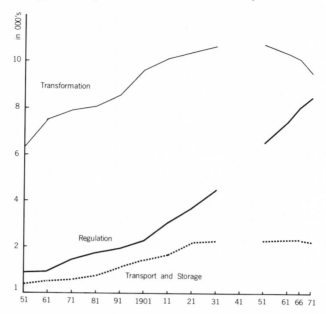

Figure 10.2. Human energy sectors of Great Britain, 1851–1971, in absolute numbers. (*Source:* Occupational tables of decennial censuses.)

The early parallel increase in human and nonhuman energy is particularly interesting. Because the economic analyses of labor have almost always separated the agricultural from the industrial workers (that is, the primary from the secondary sector), the particular trajectory of the total labor force has been obscured. That *labor as such* (here defined as the TR component) began a relative decline at this time is an important change in the dynamics of the evolutionary process. It seems likely that in the early phase of industrialism there was initiated a myth that industrial development makes jobs. At that time it was also objectively true that it did make jobs. But it is also objectively true that, beginning much earlier than has usually been thought, the increasing use of nonhuman energy began to take away jobs. The myth, however, has been perpetuated and is still used today. The opposite myth, that the machine – the popular symbol for what here is seen as nonhuman energy – displaced labor, also began to emerge. In reality, the industrialization process was not at all even, and there had been periods of immense unrest earlier when particular industries were displacing labor. Handloom weavers and framework knitters were displaced at the end of the Napoleonic era by industrial growth (Hobsbawm 1969:90–1), but the process had been anticipated in the late eighteenth century and marked by the advent of the Luddites and later in the 1830s and 1840s by the Chartists.

Whatever the fluctuations may have been before the period of the present study, the 1870 era is of major importance because it marks the final downward turn of the portion of the population that is going to be supported through transformational activities, be they agricultural or industrial. Of equal interest, in Table 9.2 and Figure 10.1, is that when the TR curve begins its long decline, the regulatory curve shows only a momentary reaction – possibly more an artifact of the data than a representation of real change. The significant change in the growth of the REG sector does not appear until three decades later, around 1900. What the economists have called the tertiary or service sector is, in the present analysis, divided between the REG and the MR sectors, the latter containing those people involved in direct services to individuals. The immediately visible effect of the TR downturn is in the MR sector, where for the next two decades the loss of personnel from transformational activities is reflected in a sharp growth. That, however, levels off around 1880. Thus the timing of the beginning of the steeper rise in the regulatory component at about 1900 may be seen to be a response to immediate factors other than those governing the TR and MR curves. Much of the dynamics of this regulatory increase was discussed in Chapter 9. The present material clarifies that the need for increasing regulation was a response to problems that first began with the change in the TR component itself and that it had immediate impact in the MR component. The problems engendered by the changes in both of these sectors is finally recognized by an increase of people involved in regulation. All of this, however, covers the entire period during which the nonhuman energy use was gradually leveling off to the approximate steady state that it was to maintain until the mid-twentieth century.

The gradual increase in human energy in transportation and storage between 1840 and 1930 is interesting for its contrast with the transformation sector. Table 3.2 shows that a major increase in nonhuman energy was in coal for railways and ships' bunkers. Coal was used here to move very large objects that – in Great Britain at least – had never been pushed by human beings. Although there were earlier occupations that were discarded, they were replaced with new occupations. If one sees transportation and storage as a way of preserving energy forms, and transformation as dedicated to changing them, TS may be seen as a different but related aspect of the whole issue of control of the environment. At this point, we can only observe that the increase in nonhuman energy simply did not have the displacement effect in TS that it had in TR until many years later.

This course of events shows perhaps better than anything else yet discussed how the impact of nonhuman energy change affects social structure. Although the change in nonhuman energy began around the 1870s, its impact through the human energy sectors was more like a ricochet, first deflecting the course of the TR curve, which in turn changed the MR curve, both of which in turn engendered increasingly grave problems that are finally manifested in a change in the REG sector. The leveling off of the nonhuman energy itself, then, presumably placed an increasing number of problems in the hands of the regulatory sector and led to the intensification of organization that is one of the results of decreasing resources. The intensification hypothesis of Boserup (1965) and her successors (Adams 1975, Spooner 1972, Wilkinson 1973) thus may be seen to operate through the many decades of a continuing history of an advanced industrial country.

Some might argue that the regulative sector changes were responses linked much more directly to something as gross as the numbers of the total population. However, a comparison of the REG curve with that of the total population does not support this (Figure 10.3). Instead, total population actually shows a slight slowing down of growth after 1911, a change that is totally unreflected in the REG curve, either absolutely (Figure 10.2) or on a per capita basis (Figure 10.1).

Let us return to the relation of the per capita TR curve and the nonhuman energy curve. It is extremely interesting that in Figure 10.1 the TR curve tends to decrease less rapidly in a manner that makes it seem, after 1860, to reflect a mirror image of the nonhuman energy curve. This would be of considerable interest if it could be interpreted to be a direct causal relationship between these two forms of energy. But although this may be the case in Great Britain, it is not clear that we can take it at face value. In fact, although runs of nonhuman energy data have been difficult to work up for other countries, continuing research has revealed no such mirror image for any other country (Adams in press). It seems more likely that the direct effects of nonhuman energy have to be traced through some rather complex sets of impacts and interactions. To do this requires that we be able to work with comparative material to see what paths different effects take. There seems to be little question, however, that there must be some direct impact of nonhuman energy on the TR labor force, and for the moment the mirror image of the British case seems to reflect this visually in a particularly impressive way.

Let us speculate for a moment on these processes. If the pattern of relationship between the total nonhuman energy and the human energy in the TR sector is complementary, then we might expect a similar relationship to emerge with respect to the REG and MR sectors if and when nonhuman energy began to be used seriously in those kinds of activities. It is likely that this is happening today in the REG sectors in some of the advanced Western countries; for example, computers and automation have now reduced phenomenally the number of telephone operators necessary as well as the number of machine operators in some

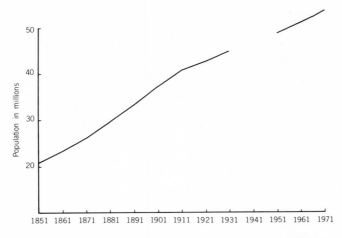

Figure 10.3. Total population of Great Britain, 1851–1971. (*Source:* Censuses.)

commercial activities. Obviously a more detailed examination of the nature of the occupational activities of contemporary society is required to explore this.

The problem is at the moment more complex with the MR sector, because we first need a much better analysis of just what kinds of human activities comprise the sector. It seems, however, that the MR sector will differ from the other two in at least one respect. It includes much human energy that people expend on themselves, such as the energy children, students, and retired people devote to their own development and living. This energy can hardly be displaced by nonhuman energy. Similarly, although some maternal activities can be displaced by nonhuman energy, it is not easy to conceive of which activities could be displaced and which could not.

Returning to our original question concerning the relationship between the change in nonhuman energy and the organization of the society, these data suggest a complementary relation between the relative size of the social sector dedicated to the transformation of nonhuman energy and the relative amount of nonhuman energy that is introduced into the system during the period under study. Speculation on the possible relation of changes in the REG sector are more tenuous, because other factors clearly come into play. Regulation seems to start up sharply a decade or two after the TR sector tends to level off. But while I would be inclined to attribute some fairly direct causal connection to the nonhuman energy–TR sector relation, I am less inclined to do so with the change in the REG sector. The principal reason for this is that moving beyond the era under examination, the sharp decline in the TR sector after World War II is not followed by any very evident change in the REG sector.

This general approach suggests that if we are to understand the real effects of increasing nonhuman energy in the society, or the change in the form of nonhuman energy, we must study specifically the manner in which it affects social processes. The macroscopic approach used here is, I believe, important as a beginning, but the research is in too early a stage to come to grips with the more precise kinds of answers we need to enlarge our understanding for practical consequences.

11. Conclusion

The late Victorian case

This inquiry started as an exploration into the interrelationships that may hold between society and changing amounts of energy. The case of late Victorian Great Britain suggests that the course of energy flows has much to do with social complexity but that the relationship is far from direct, linear, or simple. The approach has been structural, attempting to understand how the flows of energy and matter interact to release other energy flows, thereby affecting the expansion of large dissipative structures. Such dissipative processes are natural structures that are delicately balanced far from equilibrium, dependent on a complicated mixture of chemical inputs that must be kept within certain ranges for the structure to survive in a form recognizable to its constituent members. The human activities that comprise the dissipation of energy have to be seen in the context of the structures that they help to form. It is rare that the energetic consequences accurately represent the intentions of those responsible for triggering the event.

The British case was initially interesting because of the great leveling off of energy consumption in the late nineteenth century. This seemed to conform to the impression many people had about the course of British history of the time, yet (apart from its delineation by Humphrey and Stanislaw) the relationship was nowhere mentioned in the literature on the events of the period. It left in the air whether people of the time "knew what they were doing," were motivated in a direction that was good for the system. Even with the wisdom that should accompany these declining days of Western expansion, we are tempted to assume that a failure to expand is somehow bad.

Our first answer to why Great Britain gave the impression of being in some kind of decline in the latter part of the nineteenth century is that the amount of energy being consumed was decelerating on a per capita basis. The amount of work that could be called forth to accomplish tasks was declining relatively. In the fluctuating nature of dissipative structures, the effects of a decline in the ability to do work cannot be expected to be felt universally or evenly in the social fabric, and yet they must be felt somehow. They are likely to appear irregularly:

strikes, bankruptcies, loss of markets, changing distribution of income, periodic unemployment, changing occupational patterns, booms and busts, emerging social movements, and so on. The particular kind of decline that was taking place in the United Kingdom was not strictly a move into a steady state but rather into a *per capita* steady state. A full steady state would have required that the population also level off. The per capita steady state, however, would yield many of the same effects in terms of the social responses, since over the whole society, the relative amount of work being done per capita was not increasing. When a society is in full expansion, there are usually new opportunities to distract from the more disagreeable facets of change under way. A leveling off means that people are forced to draw from a relatively shrinking pie.

The second answer is that energy consumption was declining because a series of choices were made to shift the use of the energy and triggers available to British entrepreneurs and workers from the United Kingdom to other continents. Investment capital that could have been used at home went increasingly overseas; coal that could have stoked British industry went increasingly to export markets; and a hard-to-estimate quantity of human skills that might have manned private and potential government bureaucracy went abroad to seek better opportunities.

The third answer is that while these exports served in some part to bring immediate foreign exchange and to fund the import of other products, they all were destined to contribute to the construction of the larger world structure, an environment that would be hospitable to industrialization. This has been referred to here as "creating an industrial world structure." The construction of this environment was essential to Great Britain's own survival and well-being. Survival had become identified with expansion both evolutionarily and culturally. This third answer suggests that Lotka's principle was implicitly recognized and followed by many individuals in Great Britain and elsewhere. The notion that the whole process was underway to enable Great Britain to be the dominant world power may or may not have motivated some individuals, but there is little reason to expect that it operated to the exclusion of private interests. Indeed, decisions were usually based on rational considerations of self-interest, whether the individual was an experienced investor or a laborer or a politician. Diverse individuals in different classes and geographical positions saw the particiular environments relevant to them as being something quite specific. Thus laborers constructed friendly societies and trade unions and created strikes from time to time to try to force better wages, the most important element of their environment. Investors had to choose between foreign alternatives and home industries that needed expensive retooling.

These British exports acted as inputs to a series of ongoing dissipative structures abroad. They produced changes in those foreign environments and, often with British intent, changed profoundly the internal organization of the political economy, orienting some to heavy dependency on the foreign capital markets. There were also many unanticipated reactions, such as the buildup of antiforeign and anticapitalist sentiment, which would not see its full harvest for some decades, and an explosion in population, which would have the most profound consequences of all. Each diverse sector of the rest of the world was stimulated to seek its own better conditions of survival in the face of the changing exterior. The reactors of most immediate consequence to the British were the Germans and the Americans. Their expansion was the principal immediate cause of the British slow-down.

The fourth answer is that national states can most readily carry out decisions that are clearly within their power through the accepted and legitimate laws and traditions of their own societies, or through force. The only centralized decision maker that might have desired to retain Britain's industrial preeminence was the British state. Although primacy resulted from the activities of thousands of individual decisions, these decisions were not made in a systematic and coordinated way in order to achieve primacy for the nation. The trajectory of the nation resulted because the decision makers had intentions parallel or congenial to those of most of the investors and workers. That is, the preference for laissez-faire decisions with respect to government action made it politically difficult to take actions that would have very damaging effects on large segments of the population. Moreover, the British government was not sufficiently centralized. It lacked the knowledge, capability, and desire to carry out the work necessary to act precipitously with great independence. While the state did intervene increasingly in public life over the course of the century, the process was slow and reactive. The major steps in the growth of government activity were responses to critical and dangerous conditions inside the United Kingdom. The favored solution was, wherever possible, to shunt decision making to the local level. The government would not often intervene directly simply because it had not developed a bureaucratic structure to enable it to do so. In retrospect, the steps that were being taken during this era can be seen to have been building the "coral reef" of the socialized state that emerged after World War II.

The fifth answer is that given these decisions made throughout the British collectivity, and given that the growth of energy consumption on a per capita basis gradually declined to a kind of steady state, there is evidence that the society responded in those sectors where the commercial energy more directly affected the individual. Commercial energy was being used principally in industry, and it was there that industrial expansion brought an absolute increase in the number of workers; it also brought about a consistent decline in the relative percentage of such workers in the total population. The actual displacement of workers was usually indirect. The greatest decline in absolute numbers occurred in agriculture and it occurred there not because of a massive input of new energy into British agriculture but because of such an input into foreign agriculture. British grain production gave way to imported grains that were produced more cheaply abroad in the better fields and with increasing amounts of nonhuman energy. In British industry, however, the working population increased, but the effect of nonhuman energy subtly reduced the portion of the population that could be so supported.

Oddly enough, we have always assumed that such a process has taken place, but it has not been easy to demonstrate the nature of its general impact. The analysis given in Chapter 10 is, I believe, a hopeful indication that such analyses can be much further refined, and from them we can learn considerably more. The British material indicates how the larger society was acting. While British society grew, exported its people and products and money, and imported money and goods for its own consumption, the underlying pattern was to reduce the human energy being used for one kind of activity and to increase it for quite a different activity.

One way to see the change is as a shift from human energy acting on nonhuman energy and materials that constituted the major consumption in the society, to exercising controls over the triggers that determined the flow of both these goods and over the governance of human beings. Even though the shape of the REG curve (Figure 10.1) is not an obvious and simple response to either nonhuman energy change or to the decline in the TR sector, there is little question that these two processes are among the most important leading to the REG increase. It is equally important to recognize that the specific course that the REG increase took probably was answering to certain features of the British scene (as argued earlier). It cannot be concluded that the delayed regulatory growth in Britain will be repeated except in the primary industrial nations. The fact that Britain was the first country to industrialize and that it did so under an explicitly laissez-faire philosophy makes it clear that the delay clearly conformed to the British situation. In general, however, until the method used here has been further used on comparative materials, it is premature to launch into speculations on possible ramifications through the economy and society. The ramifications of how these changes in human energy sectors dedicated to different tasks affected the rest of the society must be the subject for further research.

History and explanation in an evolutionary framework

The general thesis is that history is composed of the collective product of a series of microscopic events but that history manifests a macroscopic direction. I have argued that the course of late Victorian events was partly the result of a multitude of rational decisions made by individuals in all classes of life, but the overall course of these decisions was such that it obeyed the principle of energy flow set forth by Lotka. In asserting that this mass of events behaved in accord with a general principle, we are asserting an "explanation." Explanation in evolution, however, can seldom be satisfactorily framed in terms of trying to trace the chain of lesser events that ultimately lead to a macroscopic outcome. Such a proximate approach is less than satisfactory because we can never reconstitute the events that actually occurred. We are forced to find traces of them, opinions about them, results of them, and, taking these fragments, to construct models of the past, usually based on simplistic mental constructs that we have available for such modeling. Having done this, we stand back and, with considerable uncertainty, argue that we have concocted an explanation.

The intent of this work has not been to rehash late Victorian history and punctuate it with asides about energy, explanations, and the nature of human society in general. Rather, the intent has been to argue that in explaining macroscopic events, we shall not get far by adhering to a plan that requires us to reconstruct individual events with an implicitly inductive plan of reaching some kind of "explanation." We can understand human history only by combining an approach that (1) insists that we see it as a part of larger history (i.e., that the activities of human beings are only part of a whole that includes the physical world acting in accord with its own nature) with (2) a larger theory that provides a working hypothesis as to how this larger nature works.

The present analysis is aimed at constructing a method for better understanding the nature of history. As such, it is in a vein similar to the work of Wallerstein (1974a,b) and its principal stimulus, the French school of history led by Braudel (1972). It differs in important respects, however. First, it works on the assumption that human history is a part of nature and as such must conform to the processes that dominate natural history. Thus it would label all theories that attribute cause to events described in social or psychological terms as proximate causal explanatory systems. Since it further argues that the stochastic nature of such processes makes it impossible for proximate explanations to lead to macroscopic theory, we must instead turn to selection explanations for these larger processes. For the moment, the best sources we have for the dynamics we need for the larger processes are the laws and principles of energetics. Thus this work shares with these others a concern for providing a holistic picture, but it diverges by asserting that there are dynamics more fundamental than those found in psychology, culture, or the political economy of Marx.

Some human histories in the past have erred, taking humankind to be both the generator of events and the natural selector of those actions. The position taken here is that humans are, indeed, a principal generator of events that affect them. It is in this respect that the individual decisions, the individual efforts, are crucial to an understanding of history. These individual actions have two kinds of consequences. The first is that they divert events or set them in motion. The second is that these consequences are then flooded by other events, some individually moved, but some quite nonhuman in character. Such nonhuman events include those that stem from extrahuman nature – climate, topography, seasons, the nature of the times, and in general the "state of nature." They also include the collective, conjunctive products of previous individual actions, now taking on a nonhuman quality because they are no longer a product of individual initiative. This flooding of the individually initiated events is part of the process of natural selection. The larger evolutionary pattern that is proposed here is that humankind can and does initiate (i.e., mutate, innovate, replicate) actions, but what happens as a result of those actions is instantly taken out of human hands and is determined by the concatenation, the dynamic environment, of factors into which that event inexorably moves.

Proximate explanations are less than satisfactory because they can at best only give us an incomplete and probably inaccurate model of how events come into being and because they can never give us an understanding of how those events are disposed of. They cannot do the latter because the factors that enter into the disposal of events are too multitudinous, too complex, too obscure to reconstruct. To understand the disposal, we must turn to "selection" explanations, propositions that do not pretend to detail all the antecedent factors but rather encompass a general plan or pattern of results. We can never build a plan or pattern from an exhaustive examination of the proximate events, because we do not have the methodological ability to do it. We do have the ability, however, to look at the patterning of results and hypothesize a model that will describe what happens.

We have found the course of late Victorian events to conform with Lotka's principle; this is the overall patterning of the results. This overall pattern cannot be seen if we look only at "what happened" to Britain. That is, we cannot see the map of the results if we look at only part of the scene. The operation of Lotka's principle becomes clear only when we recognize the role of Great Britain in triggering the flow of energies in many other parts of the world. By choosing to do this during the latter part of the nineteenth century, Great Britain not only chose a more effective method of increasing energy flows but also set in motion flows that were necessary to sustain its own inputs. From a sociological standpoint, this resulted in creating a new structure of energy at a higher level.

Most of this monograph has been dedicated to exploring events to see how the initiatives of individuals sought to enhance their own welfare and what some of the immediate results of this were in terms of the overall energy available to Great Britain as a nation. This statement about the overall energy available is a statement about collective results of the many individual actions. We can, for the moment, "explain" the individual events in terms of a rational theory, but we cannot explain the behavior of energy or of the British nation in terms of rationality, since that is a characteristic of individual, not collective, action. The larger patterning, that is, the decline of energy per capita in Great Britain and the increase in overall energy flow in the world at large, has to be explained in other terms, and for this we turn to the selection explanation formulated by Lotka.

The type of general theory used here is evolutionary. It proposes, however, that different methodologies are necessary if we are to examine human history in the evolutionary context. In order to examine a process that is equivalent to mutation, that is, the process whereby things are generated, it is necessary to have theories in terms of proximate events, the events that were antecedent to the events in question. Why did British investors invest abroad? Because they perceived that it yielded a better profit. Why did the Bank of England adjust exchange in order to render a favorable sterling balance? Because its job was to keep Great Britain solvent. Why did labor not demand tariff protection for industry? Because free trade was bringing prices down.

Another part of evolution is natural selection. A concatenation of events, conjunctions of disparate lines of history, come together to foster or inhibit the particular events that have been set in motion by humans. To understand these processes, we must look at selective explanations, explanations that describe a larger pattern. Natural selection, as was argued earlier, is not a deus ex machina that comes to judge. Rather, it is the totality of events, including those in question, that act together with some result. It is often possible, ex post facto, to ascertain which among the totality were more salient in a particular course of history. It is much more difficult to predict this because we seldom know what factors will be available for participation.

The approach to explaining history suggested here is, then, that different kinds of explanations must be sought, depending on the role the events play in the larger evolutionary picture. We may explain the inputs on the basis of proximate explanations; the outcomes, however, will require selection explanations.

Culture and energetics in historical explanation

Great Britain's decline from the position of industrial preeminence in the world to that of a much lesser economic and industrial power is naturally of interest not only to Britons but also to others concerned with national trajectories and the course of world history. The approach in the present study has explicitly sidestepped one of the most popular and possibly the most discussed aspect of the problem: whether the apparent decline in the late nineteenth century was due to "economic" causes on the one hand or to "cultural," or "ideological," causes on the other. Chapter 2 reviewed some of the arguments that had been brought to focus on this question, and from it three positions on a continuum can be distinguished: favoring economic processes as primary (Hobsbawm 1969); favoring cultural factors (Arnold 1913, Barnett 1972, Halévy 1951, Wiener 1981); and using an explanation based on factors of both types (Court 1965b, Landes 1969, Lewis 1978, Saul 1969, C. Wilson 1962). The recent work by Wiener probably points up the "cultural" position more explicitly than previous works, just as Hobsbawm's excellent study (1969) plants the flag most clearly for the "economic" position.

The conclusions of the present work parallel most closely the middle position, but not by eclectically combining answers from both extremes. Rather, the argument here is that the kind of theory that posed the two opposing positions is itself defective and that a solution cannot come from a synthesis worked out of a Hegelian dialectic; rather, it must come by rejecting the problem as defined. The opposing positions are more the product of the culture of the protagonists than of theories that clearly relate variables. To factor out and oppose cultural elements to the behavior of the members of the society is comparable to opposing the color of an elephant to its size. Ideas and behavior are intrinsic components of a complex process of events; neither could occur without the other. The genesis of a particular event – writing a poem or fleeing a war zone – might be ascribed predominantly to one or another factor. A long course of events, however, such as the 40-year "decline" of Great Britain, cannot be so ascribed.

The position of the present study is that this partisan dialectic itself reflects an unresolvable dualism of thinking that bunches two sets of factors that are themselves of a very different order. The contrast that is posed by some as the "technological" and "ideological" (White 1943) or the "infrastructure" and "superstructure" (Harris 1979) in fact reveals no clear theoretical relation between the two components. They claim primacy and predominance to the former but allow that "sometimes" the latter becomes primary. Matters of "economics" and "technology" are then given a special place in the historical process, and the question of "ideas" and "cultural pattern" are regarded as "secondary." There has been no acceptable theory as to just *when* the latter might become primary. The reason for this problem is that both are aspects of a series of historical events and that both play a role in every event; no human historical event has ever taken place without both in action. Indeed, the only real virtue of this now extended, polarized historical argument is that it has yielded a great deal of first-rate historical research. However, the lack of a better theory has meant that no resolution has ever been possible; and some – like Landes (1969) and Lewis (1978) – judge correctly that no such solution is possible.

The appearance of Wiener's recent work (1981) points up the issues with a particularly well done delineation of the emergence in Great Britain of a strong cultural perspective of antiindustrialism. Wiener convincingly depicts the development of a characteristically English depreciation of an "industrial spirit." Wiener's own position seems to be that the cultural side is the place to look for factors leading to British decline, although there is some ambiguity in the treatment. He opens with the statement: "The leading problem of modern British history is the explanation of economic decline" (1981:3). He then quotes Ralf Dahrendorf that Britain's "economic performance and cultural values are linked" and that "an effective economic strategy for Britain will probably have to begin in the cultural sphere" (Wiener 1981:4 quoting Dahrendorf 1976:460). But he concludes a final brief treatment of the "economic explanation" with the observation that "the question of the causes of British economic decline remains beyond the sole grasp of the economists" (Wiener 1981:170), hardly an aggressive defense of priority for the "cultural" position.

What Wiener's study does show is that there were in the later Victorian era some clear voices of discontent with the influence that industry and science had been having up through midcentury. This is well documented by such people as John Stuart Mill, Matthew Arnold, Thomas Hughes, Charles Dickens, and members of the Clarendon Commission, and it was decried by such others as Richard Cobden and T. H. Huxley. The ample evidence of the gentrification of the entrepreneur and industrialists presented by Wiener, however, and of the dominance of the traditional aristocratic perspective comes not from the nineteenth-century material but from that of the mid-twentieth century. Indeed, although he clearly shows that such ideas were abroad in the late Victorian era, there is no broad review of literature to weigh this against other positions nor to demonstrate that it was in any way dominant in that period. What Wiener does demonstrate is that this view was emerging in that era and that it had become extremely important by the second decade of the twentieth century. His account of the influence of this attitude on politics (1981:Ch. 6) is predominantly about the twentieth century, as is his chronicling of the gentrification of the industrialist (Chapter 7).

Wiener's conclusions argue:

The thrust of new values borne along by the revolution in the industry was contained in the later nineteenth century; the social and intellectual revolution implicit in industrialism was muted, perhaps even aborted. Instead, a compromise was effected, accommodating new groups, new interests, and new needs within a social and cultural matrix that preserved the forms and even many of the values of tradition. Potentially disruptive forces of change were harnessed and channeled into supporting a new social order, a synthesis of old and new. This containment of the cultural revolution of industrialism lies at the heart of both the achievements and the failures of modern British history. [1981:158]

However, the material presented does not show that such ideas "contained," "harnessed," or "channeled" industrialism; rather, it shows they were ideas that were becoming dominant *simultaneously with the slowing down of industrial expansion* in the primary industries – principally iron and steel. As is shown earlier in this study, coal production did not slow down, and other industries were coming into being. In order to designate the antiindustrial cultural values as a major proximate cause of the "decline" of British industry, one would have to demonstrate that they were *heavily* at work at least from 1860 on, because the decline begins clearly in 1870. Instead, we have a picture that shows these values to be expanding *as* industry slowed down.

The logical conclusion from Wiener's excellent study is neither that the values directly slowed down the industry nor that industrial horrors alone created the values. Rather, for reasons to be adduced, the decline of British industrial efforts relative to that of some of its major competitors began to be visible, and with this there is evidence in the literature and social events of the period that there was a growing component in the culture that denied the virtues of excessive concern with industrialism and science. The process was not one that supports either of the extremes or the middle position but rather that neither class of event would have occurred without the other. A visible relative lack of domestic success interplayed with a positive cultural attitude that other things were more important. To *describe* the course of events in this way, however, is not sufficient to *explain* why it took this direction. There are many examples of societies that publicly advertise one cultural quality yet practice quite another. Indeed, the entire Marxian argument that ideology can be used to promote certain historical directions, or that religion has been an opiate for the masses, implicitly recognize such differentiations. (See Sahlins [1976] for a recent theoretical exposition of this.)

The purpose of drawing up explanations for history is not to fix the blame or guilt on some particular historical "fact" but to construct a model with internal logical coherence that most accurately describes the trajectory of events. In the present study a much more conventional model – rational economic behavior that favored overseas investment – goes further in explaining the beginning of the slowing down of British industrial expansion than does the lack of any precise data on just how an "antiindustrial spirit" might have worked its magic. This argument holds that there were various spirits abroad but points out that it was perfectly rational for investors to invest in areas other than British industry. There was certain available rationally gained knowledge that foreign investments were much less risky and possibly more profitable than was an aging domestic industry that was encountering increasingly stiff foreign competition. One must remember that overseas activities had accounted for half a century of positive balance of payments, a fact that was surely not lost on investors. The slowing down of industry, however, certainly would have provided rational support for developing a distaste for what J. S. Mill characterized in 1848 as "that struggling to get on; that trampling, crushing, elbowing, and treading on each other's heels, which form the existing type of social life . . . ." (Wiener 1981:33 quoting Mill 1961:748–51).

Partisans of cultural explanations often forget that the description of a cultural pattern is a vast abstraction from a wide set of individually distinct human behavioral events. As such, a pattern cannot "do" anything; it cannot be a proximate cause, nor can it be used for a selection explanation. It is valuable in the present case (and Wiener does this superbly) for *describing* the emergence of such a pattern and to show that it fits logically and rationally within a society that already had such elements among its cultural antecedents. In this context, the present study shows how what happened was in fact an interplay between perfectly rational behavior and the perception of a social and international environment that was changing. This changing environment was in part – and it must always be remembered that, at best, particular proximate events can seldom be more than partial "causes" – the result of the very behaviors that were being acted out on a rational basis.

In this kind of perspective, on a more theoretical level, culture, as understood by Wiener and by anthropologists in general, may be seen as an assemblage of parts that are themselves always more groups of trees than a whole forest. Thus a description of culture always has a certain quality detached from the real events of the society, because it is always, in fact, a view of society. As such, it is only one view, and there will always be others alive in the same society. Each perspective changes as the real events evolve and as the other views shift. "Explaining" history, however, is not the same as "explaining" culture. History is a sequence of multiple events, unique and unrepeatable. Culture is a holistic pattern when taken as an abstraction and as a pattern; it cannot be an analytical tool to explain itself. Unless it is formed into a theory with dynamics, it can in no way affect events. Specific antiindustrial behaviors can affect specific events, but there is no general theory that tells us how a culture pattern affects events in general.

The use of energy as a concept in the present analysis is not arbitrary or experimental. Energy is chosen as the central analytical concept for a number of methodological reasons. First, the dominant selection explanation that we find makes sense in understanding human events is Lotka's principle, and this is a statement not about human beings but about energy flow. Thus, to understand how it works, and to employ it as a working hypothesis, we must conceive of the various human processes in energetic terms. Second, given that natural selection is not a uniquely human process but is the operation of a set of factors, many of which are nonhuman, it is necessary to have some common denominator that permits us to handle both human and nonhuman events within the same conceptual framework. An energy framework is one that makes this possible. Third, it is this quality of being a common denominator of events that is particularly useful. Although the materials in Chapters 4–9 deal very little with ideas popularly associated with energy, the choice of materials for examination is dictated entirely by the framework that distinguishes energy used in triggers from that used in substantive flows, and seeks to understand how individual decisions affected the larger flows inside Great Britain and in the outside world.

What virtue, then, does this approach have when compared with the polarized dualism of "cultural" and "economic" factors? The principal advantage is that it proposes that real events must conform with energy processes. The pattern of triggers that release substantive flows has inherently the dynamics of energy seeking equilibrium. Thus no extraneous dynamics need be called upon to explain the work done in the event. What does need explanation is why certain triggers were activated at certain times. Thus in explaining the decision to export capital in the form of individuals' skills, cash, and coal rather than to invest it at home, we turn to the argument that foreign competition and an aging and increasingly expensive plant at home made the foreign choice a better investment. The trigger actions were individual decisions that we explain in old and conventional terms of action in conformance with self-interest. Hobsbawm (1969:Ch. 9) attributes this kind of behavior mainly to capitalists; but I would in contrast attribute it to anyone in any circumstance. The government failed to trigger behaviors that would counteract this direction of capital flow because the government did not have control over triggers that were sufficient to affect those individual decisions. It required some years – the very years that industrial expansion was slowing down and that, according to Wiener, an antiindustrial spirit was ascending – for the government to build the triggers that would eventually enable them to deal directly with private capital. At this point, we can refer back to Wiener's argument and note that these triggers very likely incorporated many of the elements of the antiindustrialism that he describes.

Finally, it is probably worth mentioning that recourse to an energetic model is simply going to be odious to some scholars. There are some who feel that any use of physical models is intrinsically to have recourse to metaphors, to a "pseudoscience, with its own jargon, false analogies to physics, and cute rephrasing of commonsensical propositions." The problem is that in scanning the varieties of phenomena ranging from equilibrium objects, such as coal mines, to extremely far from equilibrium steady states, such as early-twentieth-century Great Britain, there are few, if any, absolutely natural boundaries. There are many areas where it is impossible to distinguish analogy from homology and homology from identity. The position taken in the present study is that the framework provided by energetic analysis as it is developed here asks better questions, which not only elucidate the dynamics of specific events but elucidate how those events relate to larger and more complex parts of the world process, both human and nonhuman.

In the final analysis, the question is a methodological one. If this approach brings us closer to understanding how history behaves, then the method will have served its purpose, whether it be suspect and odious or legitimate and sweet-smelling.

Advantages and disadvantages of the approach

It is important to inquire whether the effort has produced anything of particular value that permits us to judge whether it is worth pursuing further in this or other contexts. The principal consequences that appeal to me are, first, that it allows us to deal with very wide ranging phenomena within a single model that is, itself, coherent with what we know of physical processes. We do not set social science apart from physical science but see it as a special case of the latter. The model is hierarchical; the component parts are the flows of distinctive kinds of energy and the dissipative structures that form through their conjunctions. The dynamics of the movements stem from the inherent flow and structural characteristics of distinctive energy forms.

This entire approach is made possible by the dissipative structure concept and was not possible before it became available. Before its advent, this area was stymied in the development of the so-called systems theory, which in fact contained little theory but was rather a collection of concepts trying to find replicative elements in the structures of the world. It was also inhibited by the popular understanding of the second law of thermodynamics, which saw that process as one essentially of decline, of wearing out, and of having no potential for explaining the expansion of more complex structures. Far-from-equilibrium processes have made it possible to interrelate the notions of hierarchical structures, that is, apparently, replicated inclusive systems, to the dynamics of the second law of thermodynamics.

The aspect of the present approach that stems from this is to assert that human societies and organization expansion comprise a single process. Cultural evolution and biological evolution must be seen as a single expansive and adaptive process. In order to do that, human activity must be seen within the same universe of analysis as the nonhuman elements, and the concept of energy enables us to do this. Since all human activity is work and much of it triggers energy for further work, we can more easily see it as one with the nonhuman energy forms. The issue is that over the course of human evolution, human and nonhuman energy have been substitutable, and continue to be so. Thus it is important that we have a model that not only makes this substitution possible but seeks to clarify what the terms of substitution may be.

Second, the analysis draws much more attention than has antecedent literature to the fact that the construction of industrial Britain resulted in the inputs that facilitated and contributed to the construction of an industrial world structure. More important, the energy flows that accomplished these two tasks were one and the same. The competition that appeared from the United States and Germany were not deus ex machina forces that somehow interrupted Britain's world supremacy in industry and trade; rather, they were the necessary result of the success of Britain's expansion. Industrial Britain could not have continued to build itself in the nineteenth century without also building the external structure that, through its own growth, turned to constrict the British growth. This is a fundamentally ecological argument that uses energy as the principal vehicle of analysis.

Third, this approach makes clear that we can never afford to ignore the decisions and actions of individuals. They are the principal triggers in human society, if not the only ones or the most important ones. Contrary to some notions, the "energy approach" to social process is not an overwhelming deterministic model, but rather one in which we try to more accurately place the human decision-making activity in its proper perspective. The cultural phases of evolution have at critical times been determined by individual decisions, and it is of utmost importance that analysts be aware of the conditions and circumstances that may again place such decision at crucial points of change.

Fourth, with this recognition of the role of the decision and its maker, the approach also draws attention to the central role of natural selection as a process that is usually composed of too many elements to allow satisfactory analysis. The course of selection, unlike that of human decision making, has some overriding deterministic aspects, although they are by no means driven by a "prime mover" or single factor. The determinism of natural selection results from the effects of decisions on the environment – both social and nonsocial. Every human act has an environmental consequence; and these accumulate and interact within the environment so that an act produces at every point a slightly different confrontation than it did before. The changing environment contains its own dissipative structural phases and components. The human species cannot expect ultimate and continuing success apart from constructing an environment that can itself live and survive. This is not a new idea and has long been advocated by ecologists. The issue here is that it is extremely relevant to the human condition, as it has been at all points in our history. Any theory of the human condition must, therefore, not only allow for it but incorporate its dynamics. This, I believe, is the case in the present approach. This fourth virtue is, then, derivative of the second.

There are, of course, disadvantages to the approach, and these should also be detailed insofar as I am aware of them. First, it can best use new data that are either very difficult to obtain or often not available. At every point, I had to depend on data that were originally gathered for other purposes and were therefore seldom entirely appropriate to my needs. At best, I had to deal with approximations. This is a serious defect, for the economy of research may well dictate that an approach that requires such different data will not be allowed to flourish in a system of social science that is already highly developed in other directions. Natural selection may keep it from developing to a point at which it might yield more precise formulations.

Second, many of the formulations are as yet far too general to be of any immediate use. The precision of formulation that is necessary requires, in addition to better data, further development of the model. Detail is important because more useful formulations can emerge only in terms of precise statements. Areas where this is obvious include the following: (1) Regulation needs to be analyzed further. It is very complex, and its activities are much too grossly handled here. (2) The relation between human energy expenditures and its substitutability with nonhuman energy forms is a crucial problem area. Coal became important because it displaced human energy, and we are searching today for ways in which we can resubstitute human energy for petroleum and other nonhuman forms. (3) The numerous processes whereby energy flows build structures need direct attention. This is central for the kind of detail that is crucial for useful analyses. Much of the material available in economic studies is quantitative and therefore gives the impression of being much more precise than is possible in sociological data.

Third, what for me is a virtue of the analysis may prove to be an obstacle to others. Most people do not want to conceive of human beings in the same framework and terms as those used for nonhuman forms. Part of the survival equipment of every society has been to see itself as the separate, special event that is the object of survival. Many so-called primitive societies recognized that such survival rested in a careful care of the environment. No modern society adequately recognizes this because the threat from other societies has systematically displaced the importance of the natural environment in our consciousness. This is crystallized in the philosophies of all nation-states. The cultural form of social organization that separates humans from other species has proved successful in adaptation and survival for some millennia and today dominates our thinking. Obviously, the present approach is concerned that we understand the implications of this. The defect, then, is not in the approach in this instance but in the nature of human society. The approach implicitly urges that we gain the sophistication that marked our "primitive" predecessors.

Appendix: Obtaining human energy sectors

The reader must be cautioned that this analysis is based on a method that is still in fairly early stages of work development and that before more extensive interpretative use may be made of it, it is necessary to do similar studies of other countries. It is presented here because I am fairly confident that the data (saving the exceptions discussed herein) are sound, and they seem quite clearly to suggest that there was an effect felt by the change in nonhuman energy. Adams (in press) presents a fuller analysis, with comparative material from eight other countries. Work is in progress on an even broader comparative body of material.

Obtaining data on these categories rests entirely with the occupational classifications in the censuses. The industrial classifications are less preferred because they do not denote what persons spend their energy doing but rather denote to which industrial category the effort is assigned. There are many problems attendant on the use of occupational categories that will be familiar to anyone who has tried to make comparative analyses with them. In the case of the British material, the categories have changed with every census, and rather major changes have been made from time to time. Each census from 1851 on tries to lump the individual occupations into larger categories for convenience of handling, but the concepts that lie behind both the individual categories themselves and the lumping into larger units change over the years. The study of these changes is itself a revealing sociological experience, but one that cannot detain us here. There are some specific problems that arise in the British material but that are not limited to it.

The data for this work were taken from the individual censuses of Great Britain (England, Wales, and Scotland) beginning in 1841.

The categories used in each census often differ from those in each preceding census. It was necessary, therefore, to analyze separately the occupational classification used in each census and attempt to achieve a consistency of usage.

There are some problems that cannot be resolved on the basis of the kinds of data provided in the censuses. First, almost no account is taken of women and children who may be helping in family TR tasks, which was common in rural households. Although a few censuses did account for this, most did not; to have

127

included it in some but not in others would have introduced a serious disorder in the data. Thus the convention has been followed to categorize women as "economically inactive" unless they are specifically listed as having an "economic" occupation. In doing this I am not accepting the implied judgment that the women in question did no work. In fact, the classification unquestionably biases the total number of people classified in the TR sector. In some instances, the decline is probably greater than implied by the real numbers, because women and men stopped farming simultaneously when they left rural life. On the other hand, women in factories were usually so counted and the bias is not present there.

In the analysis of REG activities, a problem arises in that regulatory activities are often only one phase of the behavior of a given individual. Since human beings are themselves dissipative structures, they contain their own control processes that cannot readily be differentiated in an analysis of this kind from the rest of their behavior. So it is with the social processes. In nonhierarchical societies, all adult individuals play some role in the regulatory mechanism. Decisions that are made on the basis of consensus use the human energy of all the individuals involved. Thus if we were to differentiate a REG sector in such a society, we could not do it on the basis of occupational distinction but rather in terms of the number of hours per day or week that the individual dedicates to making decisions. Obviously that would be difficult, without even confronting the problem that many decisions are made while people are also engaged in caring for other people or in transforming natural resources into usable goods. As a result, we categorically do not differentiate regulatory activities from a sector when they are specifically dedicated to that sector. Thus, while it would be possible to separate industrial managers from others engaged in industry, and farm owners from others engaged in farm work, and then to categorize these managers and owners as part of the REG sector, I do not do so. The convention is followed of including these individuals as part of the TR sector. The same convention is followed in the appearance of administrators in MR sectors, such as in education and medicine. They are not separated from the MR sectors.

So that the reader may see more clearly the nature of the classification, the following list indicates the kinds of allocations that were made from the census occupation data to the categories used herein.

> *Transformation (TR) sector:* All classes of workers, managers, and operators in agriculture, fishing, mining, forestry, and all classes of manufacturing of material goods.
>
> *Regulatory (REG) sector:* All public administration personnel; all military, naval, and other defense and war personnel; certain professions, such as clergy, lawyers, journalists, writers, scientists, engineers, painters, ar-

chitects; all commercial activities, dealing in goods, finance, advertising, etc.; all clerical activities that are not otherwise included within the TR, TS, and MR sectors.

Transport and storage (TS) sector: All activities having to do with the transport of goods and people; all activities having to do with communications, such as telephone, telegraph.

Maintenance and reproduction (MR) sector: All people listed as economically not active (in census definitions), together with certain professions; technicians, operators and support personnel in medicine and health, social work, hotel/restaurant/drinking establishments; actors and musicians, sports persons, and domestic servants and personal services of all kinds.

References

Abramovitz, Moses, and Vera F. Eliasberg. 1957. *The Growth of Public Employment in Great Britain.* Princeton University Press.

Adams, Richard N. 1975. *Energy and Structure: A Theory of Social Power.* Austin: University of Texas Press.

    1981. "Dynamics of Social Diversity: Notes from Nicaragua for a Sociology of Survival." *American Ethnologist* 8(1):1–20.

    In press. "The Emergence of the Regulatory Society." In Jack Gibbs, ed., *The Future of Social Control.* Los Angeles: Sage.

    In preparation. *Society as Energy Structure.*

Aldcroft, D. H. 1964. "The Entrepreneur and the British Economy 1870–1914." *Economic History Review,* 2nd series, XVII:113–35.

    1970. *The British Economy 1870–1939.* New York: Humanities Press.

Aldcroft, Derek H., ed. 1968. *The Development of British Industry and Foreign Competition 1875–1914.* University of Toronto Press.

Arnold, Matthew. 1913. *Culture and Anarchy.* New York: Macmillan. (First published 1869.)

Ashworth, William. 1960. *An Economic History of England 1870–1939.* London: Methuen.

Baker, J. R. 1938. "The Evolution of Breeding Systems." In G. R. de Beer, ed., *Evolution: Essays on Aspects of Evolutionary Biology Presented to E. S. Goodrich on His Seventieth Birthday.* London: Oxford University Press.

Barnett, Corelli. 1972. *The Collapse of British Power.* London: Methuen.

Bartlett, C. J., ed. 1969. *Britain Pre-eminent: Studies of British World Influence in the Nineteenth Century.* London: Macmillan.

Bateson, Gregory. 1979. *Mind and Nature: A Necessary Unity.* New York: Dutton.

Beer, Samuel H. 1969. *British Politics in the Collectivist Age.* New York: Vintage Books.

Belloc, Hilaire, and Cecil Chesterton. 1911. *The Party System.* London: Stephen Swift.

Bennett, M. K. 1954. *The World's Food.* New York: Harpers.

Berg, Charles A. 1978. "Process Innovation and Changes in Industrial Energy Use." *Science* 199:608–614.

Booth, Charles. 1889–91. *Life and Labour of the People in London,* 3 vols. London: William & Norgate.

Boserup, Esther. 1965. *The Conditions of Agricultural Growth.* Chicago: Aldine.

Bowley, Arthur Lyon. 1937. *Wages and Income in the United Kingdom since 1860.* Cambridge University Press.

Braudel, Fernand. 1972. *The Mediterranean and the Mediterranean World in the Age of Philip II,* 2 vols. New York: Harper & Row.

Brown, A. J. 1965. "Britain in the World Economy 1870–1914." *Yorkshire Bulletin of Economic and Social Research* XVII:46–60.

Brown, Ernest Henry Phelps, and Margaret H. Browne. 1968. *A Century of Pay: A Course of Pay and Production in France, Germany, Sweden, the United Kingdom and the United States of America, 1860–1960.* London: Macmillan; New York: St Martins Press.

Cairncross, A. K. 1953. *Home and Foreign Investment 1870–1913.* Cambridge University Press.

Carneiro, Robert L. 1970. "A Theory of the Origin of the State." *Science* 169(3947):733–738.

Chapman, Peter. 1975. *Fuel's Paradise.* Harmondsworth: Penguin Books.

Clapham, John Harold. 1932. *An Economic History of Modern Britain,* vol. 2. Cambridge University Press.

Clark, Colin. 1957. *The Conditions of Economic Progress,* 3rd ed. London: Macmillan.

Cole, G. D. H., and R. W. Postgate. 1963. *The Common People 1746–1946.* New York: Knopf. (First published 1938.)

Conrad, Alfred H., and John R. Meyer. 1965. *Studies in Econometric History.* London: Chapman & Hall.

Cottrell, Fred. 1955. *Energy and Society: The Relation between Energy, Social Change, and Economic Development.* New York: McGraw-Hill.

Court, W. H. B. 1965a. *British Economic History, 1870–1914: Commentary and Documents.* Cambridge University Press.

⸻ 1965b. Review of Charles Kindleberger, *Economic Growth in France and Britain 1851–1950* [Cambridge, Mass., 1964] in *Economic History Review,* 2nd series, XVIII:432–3.

Dahrendorf, Ralf. 1976. "Europe: Some Are More Equal." *Listener* 96:458–60.

Dangerfield, George. 1966. *The Strange Death of Liberal England.* London: MacGibbon & Kee.

Darmstedter, Joel, Joy Dunkerly, and Jack Alterman. 1977. *How Industrial Societies Use Energy: A Comparative Analysis.* Published for Resources for the Future. Baltimore: Johns Hopkins University Press.

Deane, Phyllis, and W. A. Cole. 1967. *British Economic Growth 1688–1959.* Cambridge University Press.

Desai, Ashok V. 1968. *Real Wages in Germany 1871–1913.* Oxford: Oxford University Press/Clarendon Press.

Douglas, Paul H. 1966. *Real Wages in the United States 1890–1926.* New York: Kelley.

Ensor, R. C. K. 1936. *England 1870–1914.* Oxford: Oxford University Press/Clarendon Press.

Fores, Michael. 1971. "Britain's Economic Growth and the 1870 Watershed." *Lloyds' Bank Review* 99:27–41.

Georgescu-Roegen, Nicholas. 1975. "Energy and Economic Myths." *Southern Economic Journal* 41:347–81.

Habakkuk, H. J. 1962. *American and British Technology in the Nineteenth Century.* Cambridge University Press.

Halévy, Elié. 1951. *A History of the English People in the Nineteenth Century,* 2nd rev. ed., vol. 5, *Imperialism and the Rise of Labor.* London: Benn. (First published 1949.)

Hanham, H. J. 1976. *Bibliography of British History 1851–1914.* Oxford: Oxford University Press/Clarendon Press.

Harris, Marvin. 1979. *Cultural Materialism: The Struggle for a Science of Culture.* New York: Random House.

Harrison, Fraser. 1977. *The Dark Angel: Aspects of Victorian Sexuality.* London: Sheldon Press.

Henderson, W. O. 1975. *The Rise of German Industrial Power, 1834–1914.* Berkeley: University of California Press.

Hinsley, F. H. 1962. "Introduction." In F. H. Hinsley, ed., *The New Cambridge Modern History,* vol. XI, *Material Progress and World-Wide Problems 1870–1898,* pp. 1–48. Cambridge University Press.

Hobsbawm, Eric J. 1969. *Industry and Empire.* Harmondsworth: Penguin Books.

Humphrey, William S., and Joe Stanislaw. 1979. "Economic Growth and Energy Consumption in the UK, 1700–1975." *Energy Policy* 7(1):29–42.

Hutchinson, Keith. 1950. *The Decline and Fall of British Capitalism*. New York: Scribners.

Imlah, A. H. 1958. *Economic Elements in the Pax Britannica*. Cambridge, Mass.: Harvard University Press.

Jevons, W. Stanley. 1865. *The Coal Question: An Inquiry concerning the Progress of the Nation and the Probable Exhaustion of Our Coal-Mines*. London: Macmillan.

Johnson, Richard. 1970. "Educational Policy and Social Control in Early Victorian England." *Past and Present* 49:96–119.

Jones, G. P., and A. G. Pool. 1940. *A Hundred Years of Economic Development in Great Britain (1849–1940)*. London: Duckworth.

Katz, Friedrich. 1981. *The Secret War in Mexico: Europe, the United States and the Mexican Revolution*. University of Chicago Press.

Kennedy, W. P. 1974. "Foreign Investment, Trade and Growth in the United Kingdom, 1870–1913." *Explorations in Economic History* 11(4):415–44.

Keohane, Robert, and Joseph S. Nye, Jr. 1975. "International Interdependence and Integration." In Fred I. Greenstein and Nelson W. Polsby, eds., *Handbook of Political Science*, vol. 8, *International Politics*, pp. 363–414. Reading, Mass.: Addison-Wesley.

Landes, D. S. 1969. *The Unbound Prometheus: Technological Change, 1750 to the Present*. Cambridge University Press.

Lewis, W. Arthur. 1978. *Growth and Fluctuations 1870–1913*. London: George Allen & Unwin.

London and Cambridge Economic Service. 1967. *The British Economy: Key Statistics, 1900–1966*. London.

Long, Clarence D. 1960. *Wages and Earnings in the United States 1860–1890*. Princeton University Press.

Lotka, Alfred J. 1922. "Contribution to the Energetics of Evolution." *Proceedings of the National Academy of Sciences* 8:147–154.

McCloskey, Donald N. 1971. *Essays in a Mature Economy: Britain after 1840*. Princeton University Press.

1973. *Economic Maturity and Entrepreneurial Decline: British Iron and Steel, 1870–1913*. Cambridge, Mass.: Harvard University Press.

MacDonagh, Oliver. 1958. "The Nineteenth-Century Revolution in Government: A Reappraisal." *The Historical Journal* I(1):52–67.

1961. *A Pattern of Government Growth 1800–1860*. London: MacGibbon & Kee.

1975. "Government, Industry and Science in 19th Century Britain: A Particular Study." *Historical Studies* 16:503–17.

Macdonald, D. F. 1967. *The Age of Transition*. London: Macmillan; New York: St. Martins Press.

1969. "The Great Migration." In C. J. Bartlett, ed., *Britain Pre-eminent: Studies of British World Influence in the Nineteenth Century*, pp. 54–75. London: Macmillan; New York: St Martins Press.

Margalef, R. 1968. *Perspectives in Ecological Theory*. University of Chicago Press.

Mayr, E. 1961. "Cause and Effect in Biology." *Science* 134:1501–6.

Mill, John Stuart. 1961. *Principles of Political Economy*. New York.

Mitchell, B. R. 1975. *European Historical Statistics, 1750–1970*. London: Macmillan.

Mitchell, B. R., and Phyllis Deane. 1962. *Abstract of British Historical Statistics*. Cambridge University Press.

Mitchell, B. R., and H. G. Jones. 1971. *Second Abstract of British Historical Statistics*. Cambridge University Press.

Mowat, Charles Loch. 1955. *Britain between the Wars*. London: Methuen.

Mulhall, Michael G. 1899. *The Dictionary of Statistics*. London: Routledge.

Murray, A. Victor. 1962. "Education." In F. H. Hinsley, ed., *The New Cambridge Modern His-*

tory, vol. XI, *Material Progress and World-Wide Problems 1870–1898,* pp. 177–203. Cambridge University Press.

Musson, S. E. 1965. "A Balanced View." *Economic History Review,* 2nd series, XVII.

Olson, Mancur. n.d. "The Political Economy of Comparative Growth Rates." (Mimeo.)

Orwin, Christabel S., and Edith H. Whetham. 1964. *History of British Agriculture 1846–1914.* London: Archon Books.

Parris, Henry Walter. 1969. *Constitutional Bureaucracy: The Development of British Central Administration since the Eighteenth Century.* London: George Allen & Unwin.

Pattee, Howard H., ed. 1973. *Hierarchy Theory.* New York: Braziller.

Peacock, Alan T., and Jack Wiseman. 1961. *The Growth of Public Expenditure in the United Kingdom.* Princeton University Press.

Pelling, H. M. 1968. *Popular Politics and Society in Late Victorian Britain.* London: Macmillan; New York: St Martins Press.

Pianka, Eric R. 1978. *Evolutionary Ecology.* New York: Harper & Row.

Prigogine, Ilya. 1967. *Introduction to Thermodynamics of Irreversible Processes.* New York: Wiley.

Prigogine, Ilya, Peter M. Allen, and Robert Herman. 1977. "The Evolution of Complexity and the Laws of Nature." In Ervin Laszlo and Judah Bierman, eds., *Goals in a Global Society,* pp. 1–63. New York: Pergamon Press.

Putnam, P. C. 1953. *Energy in the Future.* New York: D. Van Nostrand.

Putnam, Robert D. 1976. *The Comparative Study of Political Elites.* Englewood Cliffs, N.J.: Prentice-Hall.

Rostow, W. W. 1948. *The British Economy of the 19th Century.* London: Oxford University Press.

Rowntree, B. Seebohm. 1902. *Poverty: A Study of Town Life.* London: Macmillan.

Sahlins, Marshall D. 1960. "Evolution: Specific and General." In M. D. Sahlins and E. R. Service, eds., *Evolution and Culture,* pp. 12–44. Ann Arbor: University of Michigan Press.

  1972. *Stone Age Economics.* Chicago: Aldine-Atherton.

  1976. *Culture and Practical Reason.* University of Chicago Press.

Saul, S.B. 1960. *Studies in British Overseas Trade 1870–1914.* Liverpool University Press.

  1965. "The Export Economy of 1870–1914." *Yorkshire Bulletin of Economic and Social Research* XVII:5–18.

  1969. *The Myth of the Great Depression,* Studies in Economic History. London: Macmillan.

Semmel, Bernard. 1968. *Imperialism and Social Reform: English Social-Imperial Thought, 1895–1914.* Garden City, N.Y.: Anchor Books. (First published 1960 by George Allen & Unwin.)

Shannon, Claude, and W. Weaver. 1949. *The Mathematical Theory of Communication.* Urbana: University of Illinois Press.

Simon, Herbert A. 1969. *The Sciences of the Artificial.* Cambridge, Mass.: MIT Press.

Simon, Matthew. 1967. "The Pattern of New British Portfolio Foreign Investment, 1865–1914." In J. H. Alder, ed., *Capital Investment and Economic Development,* pp. 33–70. London: Macmillan; New York: St. Martins Press.

Skinner, B. F. 1981. "Selection by Consequences." *Science* 213(4507):501–4.

Slesser, Malcolm. 1978. *Energy in the Economy.* London: Macmillan.

Spooner, Brian, ed. 1972. *Population Growth: Anthropological Implications.* Cambridge, Mass.: MIT Press.

Stearns, Peter N. 1969. "Britain and the Spread of the Industrial Revolution." In C. J. Bartlett, ed., *Britain Pre-eminent: Studies of British World Influence in the Nineteenth Century,* pp. 7–30. London: Macmillan.

Stinchcombe, Arthur L. 1978. *Theoretical Methods in Social History.* New York: Academic Press.

Taylor, A. J. 1968. "The Coal Industry." In Derek H. Aldcroft, ed., *The Development of British Industry and Foreign Competition 1875–1914,* pp. 37–70. University of Toronto Press.

1972. *Laissez-Faire and State Intervention in Nineteenth Century Britain,* Studies in Economic History. London: Macmillan.

Thomas, Brinley. 1967. "The Historical Record of International Capital Movements to 1913." In J. H. Adler, ed., *Capital Movements and Economic Development.* London: Macmillan; New York: St Martins Press.

1973. *Migration and Economic Growth: A Study of Great Britain and the Atlantic Economy,* 2nd ed. Cambridge University Press.

Wallerstein, Immanuel. 1974a. *The Modern World-System: Capitalist Agriculture and the Origins of the European World-Economy in the Sixteenth Century.* New York: Academic Press.

1974b. "The Rise and Future Demise of the World Capitalist System: Concepts for Comparative Analysis." *Comparative Studies in Society and History* 16(4):387–415.

Waltz, Kenneth N. 1975. "Theory of International Relations." In Fred I. Greenstein and Nelson W. Polsby, eds., *Handbook of Political Science,* vol. 8, *International Politics,* pp. 1–85. Reading, Mass.: Addison-Wesley.

White, Leslie S. 1943. "Energy and the Evolution of Culture." *American Anthropologist* 45:335–56.

Wiener, Martin J. 1981. *English Culture and the Decline of the Industrial Spirit, 1850–1980.* Cambridge University Press.

Wilkinson, Richard. 1973. *Progress and Poverty: An Ecological Model of Economic Development.* London: Methuen.

Wilson, Charles. 1962. "Economic Conditions." In F. H. Hinsley, ed., *The New Cambridge Modern History,* vol. XI, *Material Progress and World-Wide Problems 1870–1898,* pp. 49–75. Cambridge University Press.

Wilson, Edward O. 1975. *Sociobiology: The New Synthesis.* Cambridge, Mass.: Harvard University Press/Belknap Press.

Yeo, Stephen. 1976. *Religion and Voluntary Organisation in Crisis.* [London]: Croom Helm.

Young, G. M. 1936. *Victorian England: Portrait of an Age.* London: Oxford University Press.

Index